Using Time

Most people worship speed because they think it saves time. Most people disdain patience because they think it wastes time.

Yet what good is saving time without the clarity of mind to enjoy it? And what good is going fast without the still mind to implement it? Just what are people saving time for?

Within the Sphere of the Rolling Mirror most people don't know how to use time but are instead used by it. They try to speed the coming of the good and forestall its leaving. Conversely, they try to forestall the coming of the bad and speed its leaving. So they are often out of sync with the rolling of the Mirror. They wonder why this approach seldom works.

You see, they know well how to hurry, and they know well how to drag their feet; yet still they seem blind to the Very Middle. Somehow they forget that slowness is secondary to action. For to do something truly well goes far beyond mere results; to do a thing well is to do it with the clarity of stillness within and the action of the flow without, from start to finish.

The Sphere of the Mirror is both a turning and a Returning. It's best not to tamper with that too much. Once again, we see that the turning with the Mirror is the Highest Way.

Few see the drawbacks to both speeding and forestalling. The drawbacks are losing the Greater Flow. The advantages are only ambition and gain, things which inevitably fade.

Here's another way to put it. After he returned to the plains from the high peaks, the Man Who Returned once said, "There is clear mind, and then there is fast mind; these are surely the big and the small of it, the insightful and the confused.

"There is flowing mind, and then there is lagging mind; these too are the big and the small of it, the insightful and the confused. To sacrifice the big for the small is folly, yet we see it happen all the time. Few know how to use time but are instead used by it. They don't yet know about the virtue of neither hurrying nor dragging one's feet."

The old ones must have known something when they said, "Fast is slow. Slow is fast." And even today some will ask, "If you didn't have time to do it well the first time, how come you have the time to do it over?"

Still, most just cry, "C'mon! Hurry! Hurry!" And that's when to have patience. Settle down. Just be cool, calm and collected. Act from out of Stillness. Be careful. Use time. Don't swap the big for the small.

— from the book, Life in the Rolling Mirror.

MAVERICK SUTRAS

G. BLUESTONE

Avant Press

CONTENTS

INTRODUCTION

There are a lot of books about achieving excellence. This book, however, is about discovering the principles which underlie excellence in every activity, and in any and all fields, while crafting a deeper and richly satisfying life. Cosmic Craftsmanship.

Twelve hundred years ago a Chinese sage named P'ang Y'un recited this verse:

> My daily activities are not so strange
> It's just that I'm naturally in sync with them.
> Grasping at nothing, shunning nothing,
> Every moment no hindrance, no conflict....
> My magical power and mystical activity –
> I draw water and carry wood.

That's the way to do things! That's the way to close a business deal, paint a house, discover a new vaccine, ski down a mountain, cook a meal, or cut with a sword. That's the Way and it's the best way to do anything, or nothing at all.

In every field of endeavor there are some who seem to pass beyond mere technical expertise into another, freer realm entirely. They find a way to live which sustains their vision, and a way to look at things which sustains that deeper life. They've managed to transform their activities into a spiritual practice. Into a life of depth. Maverick Sutras is about hand-crafting that deeper life, about mastering your activities without being mastered by them.

The most skillful sort of general and the most skillful sort of janitor (or athlete, or CEO!) have more in common than the highest sort of general has with that next class of brass. It's true! Not just those with technical brilliance but those with a deep understanding born from the practice of their chosen craft.

What, then, do they share? Are there ways to look at things which infinitely broaden your world? Are there ways to do things which lead not merely to excellence but to a deepened sense of existence and flow? Are there ways to get things done, yet in a cool, unhurried fashion, in a sage-like way of action? Let's find out!

Sometimes in the following chapters we refer to the world as the "Rolling Mirror" because it's constantly in motion, and it clearly and immediately reflects our own mental state. In other words, when we are confused, the world also seems confused; when we are clear the world also seems clear. Rolling with the Mirror means to flow easily with the phenomenal world like P'ang Y'un.

The sphere of the "Rolling Mirror" is our home. It's also our school, hospital, arena, and lots of other things. A sphere of perpetual motion, the mirror is a realm where nothing can be described without using opposites.

A hypnotic, rolling wheel where relativities and appearances can easily predominate. Some call it illusion. Others call it reality. A perfect place in which to practice! But ... not always an easy one. If you want to go to sleep, this is "The Place." And it's easy to go to sleep for quite a while. In fact, if you're not careful, you might blink your eyes and nod your head, only to find that years have passed in the interim.

Yet, sooner or later we get tired of sleepwalking. The only problem is that we usually want to "do" something about it, and doing more things while we're sleepwalking just isn't the answer. If we just start doing, going, we might sleepwalk ourselves to the wrong side of town.

So, there's the sphere of the Rolling Mirror *and* the paradox and difficulty of practice. It's really a quandary. But in what we call "Practice" there's no problem at all!

We just need to wake up. We've had enough sleep! But what does that mean? To become *clear*. But what does *that* mean? To awaken, to become clear, is to begin to see the Rolling Mirror without opposites, yet to retain those opposites for reference when useful. To simply cease always pitting one thing against the other. To live without being forever hypnotized by appearances. Then see what happens – you'll be surprised!

Do it once, and it's like opening your eyes for a moment in the night. Do it twice and you'll never be completely the same again. But – soon you'll be back asleep anyway. Do it continually, over and over, *returning, remembering*, picking up the thread when you lose it –

that's the big "Practice" of living in the sphere of the Rolling Mirror.

What, really, do we mean by "Practice"? Sounds kindof boring or contrived or rigid....

Well, for the purposes of this book, "Practice" means to allow your life to be infused with depth and richness, not by chance, not through grasping at this or that experience, however new or exotic, but rather continually, through each and every experience. And through the absence of experience too!

It's very simple but not easy. It's practice because of it's continual nature, but just because of that continuity, practice can easily become stale, repetitive — even more limiting than no practice at all! So, great care is required. It's like walking a tightrope, or balancing over an abyss. To balance tension and slackness, concentration and diffusion is not easy! But that's just what has to happen before practice becomes Practice.

You may be a student of Zen, of martial arts, or Yoga, or even biology or mathematics. Or maybe you have no formal study at all! It doesn't matter. Because all practice, in a sense, is personal practice, just as all eating, no matter how large the group dining, is personal eating. Each must chew, swallow and assimilate for oneself. So too, each must establish the format for a life of Practice.

No matter how many books you've read; no matter how many hours you've meditated; no matter how many disciplines you've studied — or not studied! No matter how many teachers you've had — or how many students — it's not "Practice" until it's omnipresent in your life, until it touches each and every part of your existence. Until your practice assimilates "you" and your dated ideas of who you are. Until you and your practice become one. Until then.

And there are more formal practices than one can try or know, yet they are not necessarily what we call big Practice. They're often just a format, a shell. Big Practice is much more than a shell — it's to touch and enter the "Voidness" within that shell — it's to bloom like flowers, flash like lightning, flow like a stream. It's to *Be It!*

To live a life of Practice, and especially to maintain it alone, is not easy. In fact, it's one of the most difficult things to do. It's fraught with obstacles, with pitfalls. But that's what makes it interesting. What is Practice? It's hard to define. And harder to do. But think seriously about *this* before you begin: Just what's the alternative?

So for a day, or better still for a life, let's make a practice of finding out, intimately, just what Practice really is. Let's look closely at some of it's basic elements. Let's look together at Depth, Clarity, Flow, Wonder, Action, *and something more....*

PRACTICE

Where Am I Headed?

A simple exercise in foresight ... yet nothing that you ever do will be more important. A simple exercise, a reflection on your life as it is, and will be ... yet few acts have the power to change your life, its quality and direction, as this one.

Look at the road you're on. Where do you see it leading? If you continue to follow this road that you have taken, how do you see your life evolving over the next five, ten and twenty years? Who will you be? Where will you be? What will you see?

A simple exercise, but take your time. Look clearly, like a navigator reading a course, studying charts. The kind of knowledge that you'll glean here is the beginning of wisdom, of enlightening ... and no one can do it for you except you!

A LIFE OF PRACTICE

For us, a life of Practice is our only choice! It's not a question of "should" or "shouldn't" anymore – we have become weary of the "same old dance." *Tired of sleeping!* How ironic! So, there's nothing else for us to do, even if it's not easy, even if the habit mind can give us a hundred reasons to postpone opening our eyes wide; even if our logical mind can create a hundred arguments as to the limitations of practice, as to the duality of practice. And those reasons may be tempting, those arguments convincing, but ... *then what?* We still have to Practice, whether we practice or not, simply because we're tired of the alternative. We've "been there, done that," and it's no longer enough.

A life of practice may be dualistic – our logical mind can be right about that! But a life of Practice is not. A life of practice is usually pretty tough to maintain for a long time because it's often based on some idea of acquisition, sometimes subtle, sometimes not. A life of Practice, however, is to enter into Practice totally, to throw your entire life into the "pool of no opposites," and not worry if you'll be able to breathe. It's hard! It really is. But it's not as hard as we make it.

HIGH, MIDDLING AND NO-PRACTICE

There's practice and there's Practice. One tends to become repetitive, the other somehow remains fresh. One leads to "more of the same," though sometimes with different "clothes," the other strips those clothes away. One strengthens the mind of opposites, one re-absorbs and heals those opposites. One leads along a thin line of the future preceding from the mouth of the past, the other simply re-enters the Panorama, the depth of the limitless present. And, yet, practice and Practice are not just another pair of opposites because *one* of them easily includes the other.

It's not that they were *wrong* exactly, but the old guys made a lot of problems for everybody, stirred up a lot of confusion when they chose up sides in the muddy terrain of "sudden" and "gradual" enlightenment. More opposites! Thanks a lot!

Well, they not only muddied things up for people back then, some are slogging around in this same "suddenly gradual" mud even today. So, if you want to have a practice of some kind, of *any* kind — it's best to not be fooled by these old guys. You have to reach a point in your practice and in your life where even the most famous sages can't mislead you. You have to be sharp!

Gradually! Suddenly! Most of the time these ways of looking at things just don't go beyond themselves. As usual when we pit "this" against "that" we get a little wild. Confused.

But, in one way, at least, it's true: there's a kind of practice where you *do* things and a kind of practice where you *cease* doing things. Every practice, spiritual or otherwise, has this same division. In every tradition we find those who believe that there are things, important things, to do, and they're usually pitted tooth and claw against those who believe there's nothing to do, or nothing that can be done. Religions are usually big on this: We can either "save" ourselves through effort, practice, or we've already been "saved" so any effort is both vain and unnecessary. It's a real dilemma.

Only within the greater realm of Practice can this dichotomy be resolved. Only within Practice do opposites cease causing problems. And in order to enter this broad, vast, edgeless realm we can't take either side, or try to make both sides artificially blend together. To really enter the realm of Practice we have to simply find a way to do without doing, to do without the feeling of doing, where both doing and non-doing are both simply words, moon-pointing fingers, for the same vast nameless state of the Before. The state Before opposites have arisen. This is Practice. This is real Doing, the best way to do *anything* at all. This is the Return. This is Action from stillness.

And there's no practice, no meditation that will

make this happen. Yet we somehow have to make this leap anyway. Just loose your hold on "how," keep your opposites for reference but don't let them divide your mind. Hold them lightly! Even though you may have to ease into it *gradually,* you'll still have to see it *suddenly,* instantly, in one eye-blink. And, not just *once,* but over and over. That's the tricky part!

People like to talk about levels, stages, but really, there aren't any. Yet because people have this gaining-mind, these concepts *are* there. Like the idea of time zones — we use them for convenience, for reference, yet when people examine the earth from space no one sees them at all! So, don't try to make such things disappear, but do remember to be careful of their arbitrary nature or Practice will elude you.

Our mind of Clarity tells us that there is really nothing to do, that the mind is unaffected by change, that it is pure and bright from the beginning. And yet we're moving creatures, karmic creatures too; we like to have a format. We have to *do something!* So let us do without doing! We needn't throw out our practice, whatever it is, just let's not become deluded by it. Or even by the old guys, ourselves, or anyone else!

So just open your mind. Don't make problems where none exist. Use opposites without being used by them. *Gradually* practice with all your heart, yet throw out the extra. *Suddenly* understand. Let the opposites just be what they are. Find out what that means. That's the practice of no-practice. That's our Practice!

7

THE WAY OF ADVERSITY

Really this chapter should be "The Way of Change," but our tendency to see things in terms of likes and dislikes often makes the Rolling Mirror seem like it's bucking us, thwarting our progress toward projected goals, whether noble or base.

There's a mind which tends to see everything in terms of payment and acquisition — it's just that old familiar gaining-mind again, dressed in a different suit of clothes, maybe a little harder to spot if you're not looking for it. Sometimes, though, this gaining-mind tends to rally itself around slogans like, "no pain, no gain," or "you get out of something what you put into it," a little too vigorously.

Then, we can get a little lost. Not only will we *work* as hard as a fanatic (which might be okay), we'll *become* a fanatic (which is not okay). Then, gaining-mind runs rampant, unchecked, and yet does so with official approval (bestowed by itself).

There is the approach to Practice where we try to appropriate it, take it into the smallness of our lives. Well, only a small practice will fit into such a cramped space. Not Practice.

There's another approach where we throw our lives wholeheartedly into Practice where that limited, confined space becomes absorbed by something greater. To do this takes a great faith in the buoyancy of the Way, yet it's the most direct way for us to go beyond the narrow hallway of ordinary practice.

To trust in the Way, and move easily with change is to roll with the Mirror. It's Flow. Not just "easy" change, pleasant change, but change with setbacks, adversity too. To see both from the wholeness of your mind without pitting one side against the other will take you into the vastness of Practice immediately.

Sometimes people decide to "trade," to make "this" sacrifice for "that" result. Sometimes people even decide to do this or that austerity as a "spiritual" practice. And sometimes people *do* gain strength, physical and mental, from such practices. But, it's still just practice. For those sacrifices that we *agree* to make, that originate within the small mind of likes and dislikes, have nowhere near the power, grace, and wonder of rolling with the mirror, of adapting and responding to changing circumstances fluidly without a mental whimper.

Of course, to really do this requires the clarity to see that life is a whole, and that there's a "perfection of imperfection," a perfection that lies beyond our likes and dislikes, beyond merely getting what we want. This is to perceive the blue sky which lies continuously behind the changing, ephemeral shapes of passing clouds. This is when adversity itself becomes a Way. Becomes Practice. But not contrived adversity, agreement sacrifices. These might be practice but seldom Practice.

And when we deal with the Adverse Changer, the Rolling Mirror, with tenaciousness, determination, or with "positive thinking," that too is just practice. It's not rolling with the mirror with your "Blue Sky Mind," the mind which turns visits of the Adverse Changer into the Way. It goes beyond any contrived practice, it's *big*. It's being alive in the Now. It's to let the very fact of difficulty point out our attachment to like and dislike. It points the way to Return.

Seeking out difficulty isn't usually necessary; change will happen by itself, the Mirror *will* continue to roll. But will you? Decide to do so. Be ready. To roll with the Mirror is to discover Flow. To discover Flow is to discover The Way of Adversity. Which is really just being in harmony with the Way of Change.

PRACTICE BEFORE PRACTICE

Many people see the necessity of practice when things aren't going too well, while they're having a tough time. Then, however, it's usually too late; the mind just won't settle down. And practice often becomes tainted by "escaping-mind" or "gaining-mind." In other words, practice often becomes reduced to just a means for feeling better, or "fixing things up." Real practice, Practice, is quite different in that it exists before necessity — *before* any formal type of practice at all. True Practice precedes action itself — very few people appreciate this important point. It is a kind of *preparedness,* a preparedness which is not a reaction to circumstances, situations, but precedes them. We call this the Mind of Readiness; it's ready, and watching too, *but not for any particular thing!* It's a mind which is alert but not narrowed.

This mind, the Mind of Readiness, is both broad and alert at once, and it's the key to Practicing before practice. If we don't discover this Mind of Readiness, Practice will elude us and our formal practice, if we have one, may even delude us!

One thing we have to see in order to go any deeper with all this, is that the active, preoccupied, unready state of mind (you know!) is always on the verge, always a hair's breadth away from changing unpredictably with circumstances. So when we feel "good" mentally, we should recognize if it's just a "good" which could become "bad" in an eyeblink depending on the Big Changer, if it's a mind of calm which owes its existence only to calming circumstances, rather than to the Mind of Readiness.

For the Mind of Readiness *is* the Return itself! It's simply to return to that state before the beginning — before circumstance, especially before gaining-mind and escaping-mind muddied things up. If you know how to do this, all the various states of mind won't be able to confuse you at all. Let them come. Don't try to get rid of them — that's gaining-mind. And don't try to run away from them — that's escaping-mind.

So, the really interested student, the one who would Practice, doesn't wait for difficulties to arise. This person just keeps Returning from distraction over and over, again and again. This Return then becomes the vantage point, the benchmark from which to tranquilly observe all changes whether "inner" or "outer."

To do this we have to be pretty sharp! We have to see the moving mind for what it is. Unreliable! Precarious! Always on the verge! Its calmness is not real calmness, its happiness just a temporary effect of causes. So, be careful! Because things *will* change. Count on it.

Return. Just once. Then again. And again. But not to *get* anything and not to *escape* anything. Just Return because in your heart you begin to feel that that's where you belong. It's really just going home.

In every activity it's always best to be prepared beforehand. Yet in the all encompassing activity of living, just what does that mean? Look closely. Ask yourself. Find out.

A real plus, and a very interesting part of "Practicing before practice," is that others can't see us do it. They assume you're just doing what they're doing. If you do have a Good Friend, he or she will know, but others just won't see it. They *may* sense it, but they won't know what it is. And, *you* will only recognize it yourself by Returning, so ... Return!

Come to the before-mind, the Mind of Readiness. Return. Again and again. Look from out of the window of this mind. Act from it. Be ready, but not for anything in particular! Don't wait for difficulties to arise — try it *right now.* Stop reading a minute. Discover the Mind of Readiness. Discover Practice before practice. You'll never get tired of it!

LEARNING BY ONESELF

Learning, practicing, Practicing without a Good Friend can be very challenging at times. There's many pitfalls to watch for. Sometimes you will think that you know more than you really do; other times you think you know less than you really do! Sometimes we wallow in slackness, at other times Practice itself becomes choked off by excess tension. Finding that natural balance isn't easy — and when you *do* find it, things will soon change! So practicing alone without a Good Friend is like navigating, like sailing, like driving. It's a constant process of alertness and adjustment. You just can't be like a machine; you just can't indulge in sleepiness for too long! You have to be alive in the present!

But really, even if you have the best friend, the wisest teacher, you're really mostly on your own anyway. You still need to navigate, keep your eyes open, constantly adjust your course, and explore for yourself. If you leave it all up to the captain you won't learn much.

So, if you do happen to be on your own, trying to "eke out" a practice, trying to live a life of Practice, with no help, without depending on others, you're actually quite fortunate. If you continue, you'll discover a great power, a power for Practicing. And, of course, if you have a Good Friend, a teacher - well, you'll have even more problems to deal with. Then you may develop a strong sense of Practice by dealing with problems you never even knew you had!

But a teacher won't tell you too much, won't make you dependent. This Friend is helpful, sure, but casts you off on your own as much as possible so that you can discover the power of Practice for yourself. So, whether you have a teacher or not, in many ways you're in the same boat. So, *navigate!* And, the best way is just not to become too attached to whether it's easy or difficult waters. We may talk about "beginning and continuing," but we can't just press on blindly — we have to be alert, we have to sail our way through the sea of Practice, by *navigating*, not just setting a bearing, putting it on auto-pilot and leaving it go at that! Navigating means balancing our activities, our stillness and action, our tension and slackness. It's knowing when to do more and when to do less. Continually!

It's very common to be always wondering, asking, "What should I be doing?" Always wondering if there is something else, some other practice that would be more beneficial than what you are currently doing.

But, this is usually not the right question. For the student who would Practice, *whether they have a formal practice or not,* how they do what they do is a much more important concern. In other words, what is the quality of action and of stillness that they bring to every task, every practice? To change your focus, from preoccupation with *what* you are doing, to awareness of the *quality* with which things are done is a key to practicing, and Practicing, on your own.

Learning by yourself is not so much dependent on any specific practice as it is to discover this already existent natural attunement to our balance, our inner and outer environment, and the quality and depth of our actions, whatever those actions may be.

Another key to learning on one's own is to do things with the same intensity as if we are very serious, and yet to not take ourselves and our results very seriously at all! This is an art, an approach to life which is Practice itself. If we become attached to results we lose non-gaining-mind and then Practice goes out the window. If we take ourselves too seriously, that excess tension will hinder the Flow in our activities, and then we won't be able to understand what is meant by non-effort.

Yet non-effort, non-gaining mind doesn't mean to be lazy either! Just let your actions emerge from stillness, letting go of excess tension, excess seriousness or frivolity, and concern for results. This is what we mean when we say that *what* you do is not as important as *how* you do whatever it is you do.

Stand back a bit and listen clearly to all the "spiritual advice" abounding nowadays. Read books if you want but don't be misled by them — you have to navigate for yourself! Just doing things in this big, broad way we've been describing will insure that you don't get lost.

Especially beware of the people who say that the ego must "die." Nonsense! The ego must stop interfering! *That's all!* Why should the ego die? Its existence is questionable as it is! Thinking like that will only engage the gaining-mind. The ego, in order to practice on one's own, to Practice, just needs to recede in importance a bit. It just needs to become the secondary, rather than the primary way in which one experiences the Rolling Mirror.

So, once again it's a question of balance: don't take yourself or your task too seriously yet give it your best energy. That's good practice. It may seem like walking a tightrope in the beginning but later the very spaciousness of your mind will make it seem like a broad path with lots of room on either side.

When you live in this way, when you practice like this, your presence in the Rolling Mirror becomes quite natural and, like a flower or a tree, like a waterfall or the song of a bird, your actions have an unselfconscious beauty which enriches existence not just for you yourself but for everyone. That's when practice really becomes Practice.

It's easy to talk about yet a bit harder to do. That's because we always want to interfere. You just have to jump in and begin to feel your way. Talking about it's not enough! And although it *is* difficult, it's simple.

There's one more thing that you should know in order to practice alone and yet still keep your practice fresh: *The body thrives on rhythm yet the mind is dulled by it!* So when dealing with repetitive things be extra careful, alert. That's how to deal with routine and it's an art. There may be lots of things to be said about practicing on your own, but, really, this is all you need to know.

THE TWO-EDGED SWORD

Big Practice is the way of the Return, the way back to where you really are before confusion arises. But, it's easy to become lost, to go forth without Returning and just hang there awhile.

If your intent doesn't go beyond the narrow tunnel of practice, if you're just looking for another activity, an interesting way to spend your time — then that's not too difficult. Just do it like reading a book: begin at the beginning and then continue. Nothing much to it.

However, if you would Return over and over, enter the much larger realm of Practice, and *maintain* that vital Practice, that's quite different. You just can't "begin and continue," or you may often find that you are moving toward distraction rather than toward the mind which preceded distraction.

And, unlike walking a preset path, a hallway with few possibilities on either side, you have to be able to adjust, to *steer*. You have to be able to turn both right and left. You have to sense when to be active, when to be passive. You don't want to be like the wasp and know just One Big Thing. Because if you only have one way to deal with the ever-changing images in the Rolling Mirror your Practice may become stale. Become small practice. And then you'll become weary from trying to hold it all together. So, we may need some kind of help, some kind of tool....

Here's a sword for you, a razor sharp sword that will cut through all sorts of illusions and obstacles if you learn to wield it properly. It's the sword of the Return. Technique, perhaps, but big technique — *technique which leads beyond itself.* And, it's a two-edged sword which will cut in either direction, a sword of both action and stillness. It's a sword borrowed from the warrior-sage but anyone can use it. It will help you to Return and to maintain a life of Practice, whatever your practice may be. This two-edged sword is actually the highest form of meditation but a meditation totally beyond any system, formal name, method, or dogma. It's a sword which even cuts through the *meditator* and the meditator's *motives.* That's not bad!

One edge of your new sword cuts without even moving — it's the unbelievably sharp blade which severs all things as they blow against it. This is the edge of *"waiting,"* and it involves STOPPING, totally, within and without. It is to let both "inner" and "outer" forces build and ebb as they will. It's to allow the murkiness of the water to clear by itself as you do *absolutely nothing.* This edge of *waiting* is such a simple thing yet it allows your mind of situations, problems, and confusion to Return to its natural state. To the state before the pressure of gaining-mind interfered and distorted things.

Though this sword of waiting is passive, don't be

fooled; it takes resoluteness and real mental strength to wield it, and it will in turn free up a tremendous, unattached energy within. You'll reside in motionlessness and become that sharpest sword against whose edge all things are cut. But you must learn to calmly *wait* until the water becomes crystal clear. To *wait* without stirring anything up. Learning how to *wait* like this is a wonderful and awesome ability. People these days often become attached to all kinds of mental phenomena but, remember, these are just the going forth *not* the Return. They are all still "just more things," and not one of them is equal to this sword edge of *waiting*. Spend time with it!

The other edge of your sword, the edge *of "questing"* is quite dynamic, there's nothing passive about it. It's a true sword cut and all your energy, your entire spirit must be focused into the very edge of the blade. You have to arouse your energy — a half-hearted cut won't do. But if you learn to cut sincerely, with the power of *immediacy* this edge of inner *questing* will cut through any Gordian Knot. It will cut right through the dreamlike shell of your past, through distractions, and confusion. It's that powerful!

It's simple — but you must be *alive* to make the cut. To wield the sword of *questing,* gather all your energy for a decisive cut and then focus all that energy into a brief but *intent* search for the form of your own past. Nothing gradual about it, this is a sudden technique, an *unleashing*. This sword of questing will cut through each and every obstacle. See for yourself what happens when you search *suddenly* for the very form of your own past.

Through this cut you will Return, paradoxically, to the same clarity you found through the edge of *waiting*. Not gradually becoming clearer, though, but instantly with one decisive cut! Searching for the form of your past cuts through illusion, pierces the Rolling Mirror itself.

Tune into your own energy. Learn the "when" of it. It's like night and day, when one edge just isn't there for you, the other will be.

It's been said that the Way of Practice is easy, that all you need to do is begin and continue. But the Way of Practice is not easy, for there is a third, more difficult requirement which is to, at all costs, avoid becoming a master. Never think of yourself as a master or Practice will die on the spot.

So, if you want to maintain this life of Practice you must find some way to avoid becoming a master. It's that simple. If you can study deeply, observe closely, trust in the Flow without becoming a master, you can maintain your Practice while living a life of grace and beauty.

To be or become a master is to be or become something other than the Flow. Something other than the Present Unfolding. It's actually to move in the wrong direction.

DEPTH

Entering the Passive-Receptive

An exercise to increase sensitivity, strengthen intuition. A means of reacquainting you with your own perpetual background, with the canvas on which you paint your life....

Ancient martial artists studied this passive-receptive state in order to return to that clear, mirror-like state in which an impending attack could be perceived instantly, without distortion. In India, yogis entered the passive-receptive through listening, in order to hear the perpetual sound current taught to be omnipresent throughout the universe.

To enter the passive-receptive is to reverse the outward flow of the mind for a time. Instead of being the usual transmitter that we are, become a receiver for a change.

Listen, sense, receive. That's all. Become aware of that which is both within and without. Of the spaces between your thoughts, of the blue sky behind the clouds. Listen, as if for a sound in the night. Enter the passive-receptive ... hang out there and learn.

A LIFE OF DEPTH

What is a life of depth? Is it to have a lot of "deep" experiences? "Spiritual" experiences? "Enlightenment" experiences? Or, are we immediately off the track when we envision *any* kind of experiences which would fill a life of depth? Important questions!

To really live a life of depth is to not depend on *any* kind of experience at all — whether "profound" or not! Rather, it is to let each experience point you back to the void from which it arose, to the state present before experience itself.

To see that each experience is your own perception of conditions continually emerging from the stillness of emptiness is half of it. To be reminded by experience (rather than hypnotized by it) to Return is the other half. So to live a life of depth, experience becomes a finger pointing back to the Before. *It's a reminder.*

When, each day, you are not merely lost in the *content* of experience, but are reminded by it to Return, things change. Then the panorama of the Rolling Mirror becomes less based on appearance, the sensory surface of things, and more on the depth from which all is continually emerging. So, for us, the primary significance of all experience, whether "good" or "bad," "shallow" or "deep," is of a *reminder!*

Then, for the first time, practice becomes Practice. We can find out what *depth* means. We don't aim at cluttering up our life up with more experiences as one fills a container, but rather begin to appreciate the emptiness of the container, the essential space which allows any "filling" to begin with!

When we are not quite so hypnotized by the *content* of experience we can discover a life of depth on our own. No one needs to point it out to us. When experience itself becomes the "pointing finger," we have the necessary ingredient to live a life of depth.

We can then begin to live more and more from the deep stillness from which everything is emerging and Returning. We don't one-sidedly emerge without Returning anymore. We go on home for awhile too. *That's* deep! What are you waiting for?

LIVING THE GIFT OF TIME

If we're not careful, it's easy to see time merely as duration instead of as Existence Itself. Or merely as a string extending from past to future. We have activities, milestones, experiences — and those are merely knots in the string. The Panorama vanishes and with it goes our life of depth.

When we see time merely as duration we can only oscillate between "enduring" that duration, and distraction. The significance of our activities, *all of our activities,* may then elude us. Then things can get difficult. That's when people rush to practice; hurry up to meditate! It's just gaining-mind trying to use time for its own ends, and our life of depth can end up the victim of this small way of seeing.

It's when the duration of time gives way to the *quality* of time, to the *depth* of time that we're on the "right track." To value time as existence itself is the way of Practice, the life of Depth! Then it's the Panorama rather than the endlessly knotted string. But how does that happen? How do we suddenly see that "quality"? How do we make the leap?

Simply by not dividing our activities into important and unimportant. As long as we continue to do this, life itself, existence itself, remains distorted, remains a collection of unimportant moments punctuated with arbitrary moments of "significance." We may want to live a sacred life, a life of power and beauty but it's no longer possible. There are simply too many wasted moments, too many gaps, too many activities performed without the true power of our Being.

The illusion that there are important and unimportant moments robs us! It makes it impossible to value time as Existence, as Life. It's just an illusion created and sustained by gaining-mind.

And, until you can value each moment of the passing stream, you will not be able to Return upstream to the Source. Your stream will be unnavigable. Too many sections of it are missing!

When time is no longer merely duration, but rather the depth and richness of the Panorama, life becomes a sacrament. You needn't hurry up to meditate – each moment before and after meditation will be meditation too! When you value this great deep emptiness of the Panorama, you will value the infinite possibilities inherent within the precious vessel of time. Then there will be no unimportant moments.

To value the potency of this emptiness is to come to the Panorama. To come to the Panorama is to cease wasting time, killing time. To cease wasting and killing time is to cease dividing time up according to the dictates of your gaining-mind.

Now, how will you live the gift of time? It's up to you.

ENTER TOTALLY

Just as some might think that a life of depth is a life filled with so-called "deep" experiences, there are those who think that a life of depth is to be filled with "profound" thoughts. These people like to *think* about a life of depth, *talk* about it. But, their thinking, no matter how profound the subject, is just thinking; their talking, no matter how profound the words, just talking. This approach remains shallow because it never goes beyond itself.

Actually, a life of depth is to be *totally present* — to live close to the source of your thoughts rather than merely within the flat world of the thoughts themselves.

To be totally present means that we perform our tasks with our entire being — that we hold absolutely nothing back to weigh results or be distracted. We enter our tasks totally, like diving in water, and we become totally wet. This is when people talk about feeling "alive."

Actually anyone can learn to feel this total entry during sports, or when in danger. They speak of this extra aliveness, yet then, when their activity is finished, they revert back to the same old routine. Half there, half alive.

A life of depth, however, is to enter totally into our action regardless of what we happen to be doing. It is to become the action itself. This is not so hard as long as we give one hundred percent of ourselves! Nothing held back — this is how to squeeze every last drop from life, how to keep the container of life deep and empty. And, this life of depth does not refer solely to the deep quality of our action, but of our inaction as well!

It's easy to lose your way here, so be careful! Many people who *seem* to give everything to their work actually become ill. For them, there's nothing left over too, but not the *Nothing* that we're talking about. And, it's not the work that makes them ill, it's not the entering totally, it's the attachment to the work, and to results that makes them ill. Perhaps they are entering totally into attachment! Our way, however, is to enter so completely into our work, and every action, that there is simply no room for concern with results, no room for attachment of any kind. It's the only action with real power.

It's like a smokeless fire. It's how to give one hundred percent and have Nothing left over.

AWARENESS OF DEATH

We don't live far away from death. That's a fact! Yet it's easy to live forgetfully, as if we do. Even if we intellectually accept the fact of death, if we live as if death is really something which happens to others, then we will be excluded from a life of depth.

We usually don't know *when* we're going to die, or *how*. Those are facts too! Even if we think that we've come face-to-face with the fact of dying but project that death into the future, into certain circumstances, we've lost the awareness of death and its power. We may imagine that we will die like the old guys, the sages, who died peacefully, perhaps with a final enlightenment, or maybe teaching others right to the end. Everyone will be impressed with us! We'll have our own story.

But it might not be like that at all! We may never have a better opportunity for anything than we do at this moment. We may never have a better opportunity to be aware of death than right now! The Rolling Mirror is a sphere of change, and the Big Changer often neglects to send announcements! That's what we're talking about. So, don't confuse the *thought* of death with *awareness* of death. Don't project yourself into the future. Above all, don't wait for an invitation! It's always Right Now.

Death is the one factor which immediately puts everything back into perspective. Problems, rewards, windfalls, even "enlightenment" — everything! Awareness of death brings clarity to the mind. Unfailingly. Awareness of death is the most powerful antidote there is to gaining-mind. And, don't mistake this awareness as the way to a life of depth either. To have this awareness *is* a life of depth!

This awareness of death (and not just the mere thought of it) imparts immediacy into our lives. It's like a transfusion. A new energy flows within. Our actions acquire power for the first time. Sound okay? Sure!

But what if we can only seem to muster *the thought* of death? That's it. Then what? Then we allow that thought to complete itself. Allow it to mature. For the thought of death is one of the few thoughts that we can reliably intuit as a finger pointing at the moon, as a thought which points to something far greater than the word. We just need to intuit it. We just need to *ease* into it. Most people who practice just don't let the thought of death mature, and never make it to that tranquil awareness to which it points. They're too hasty — they're moved around too easily, too quickly by gaining-mind. Just *ease* into it. And stay with it.

So, even if you've understood nothing else so far about Practice, or even practice. Even if it all still seems pretty confusing to you, well then just understand this: You don't know when or how your life and opportunities in the Rolling Mirror will come to an end. Just that, and your life will change.

In martial arts this awareness of death is the way to

fearlessness. For every kind of practice this awareness provides us with a fresh and immediately useable energy. It's a direct line to richness, clarity and a life of depth. It reminds us that there's no time for slackness in our practice – it helps us to "get with it."

And for the very sharp person, the person who would Practice, it does something more – it's a reminder that not only is there no time to waste in laziness and inertia, *there's no time to waste on self-judgement, frustration, and impatience!* It tempers things.

So, discover the awareness of death. It *will* change your life. Just don't let gaining-mind appropriate it for its own ends. It's for Returning to clarity – not for *becoming* anything at all. Get close to it and stay there awhile. There's Nothing like it!

SPIRITUALIZING LIFE

There are so many ways to unnecessarily complicate things here in the Rolling Mirror! It's a good thing that we always have the vastness of simplicity to which to Return. The vast Emptiness of nothing-extra....

It's somehow easy for people to come to feel that the key to a spiritual life, a life with a sense of the sacred, the profound, lies in what is special, in what is exotic. Seminars of all kinds seem more potent than practice; teachers and teachings of all kinds – the more exotic the better – seem more desirable than Practice. And though it *is* possible to learn something from the special and the exotic, to value them above daily life, above the ordinary, is just delusion.

What is "special" is only the spices of practice, of living. You can't eat only spices – you must have food. All the rituals of practice too may be nothing more than flavorings. How long have we been trying to live on flavorings? If we've been doing this for awhile we may be getting a little sick by now. So we have to be our own doctor here, tap our reflexes a bit to determine if we're still alive – or, if our practice is. Really!

So, if we feel that something is missing, if we're always eating the rituals of practice, the spices of seminars and exotic lands – and yet we're still hungry – perhaps we're just not getting enough real food! If we would spiritual-ize our sense of personal existence, let's begin not merely with seasonings but rather with the sustenance of daily life. Let's reverse our focus from the special back to the ordinary, to the bricks from which our life is built. For somewhere within the ordinary, hidden in plain view, lies the profound, mysterious, spiritual existence that can be found nowhere else.

Once we understand this we finally know just where to look. And once we know where to look we begin to sense the depth within the ordinary, the wonder inher-ent within our most mundane act. Suddenly nothing seems to be hidden away at all! This is real alchemy, turning lead into gold. Then we cease dividing life up into special and ordinary, into important and unimpor-tant. We simply do everything as if it's important, as if it has value. And then it really does! Then we become Emptiness sacredly handling Emptiness.

Then you have the sustenance to spiritualize your life. It's not dependent on dogma, on ritual, even on practice. Those are just spices, seasonings, as are more seminars and more teachings. Discover the wonder within daily life, however, and that's Practice, that's a life of depth, that's *food*.

You wonder if there's a trick to all this. You're right, there is: You can only be Emptiness sacredly handling Emptiness when there is no attachment to results. When attachment arises it's easy to become lost, to become compulsion coarsely handling objects. So, watch it!

How do we have right attitude toward results? By seeing them clearly without attachment. By seeing that they are merely the *leavings* of action. They're just the tracks left behind by the horse of Emptiness. There's no need to carry the tracks around with you! When you can see it like that yet enter totally into your daily tasks; have no attachment and *yet do a beautifully crafted job anyway* — that's how to spiritualize life. Then food tastes good, spices taste good, everything's fine.

Then we can enjoy the special even more while we're being sustained by the ordinary. The mysterious and profound ordinary, of course.

THE WAY OF COMMITMENT

Let's face it: commitment to *anything* is not a common virtue these days. It somehow conflicts with modern ideas of personal freedom. And often the commitment that we *do* see is merely commitment to gaining-mind. And commitment to gaining-mind, of course, is not commitment at all but rather just plain old attachment. Apart from this "attached commitment," we'd have to say that most equate commitment with overseriousness at best and bondage at worst. That's just the way it is.

But, just as there is practice and Practice, there is commitment and Commitment. And it's vital that we understand this larger sense of Commitment if we would live a life of depth. For without it, Way is reduced to way, Practice is only practice, and a life of depth becomes shallow, an impossibility.

Within the realm of practice, commitment may be toward a certain way, or discipline, a certain teaching, or perhaps a particular style of martial art, or yoga, or a certain "type" of meditation. Maybe an ideology of some kind, or an ideal. In the always larger realm of Practice, Commitment is very different. Different because it is not directed toward things, or ways to do things, or ways to think about things, but rather to That which *precedes* things and our thoughts about them.

If we can understand the essence of this "before things Emptiness," then we can understand Emptiness in action, Emptiness in things. Then our commitment to *anything* at all takes on a different meaning. Then commitment merges in Commitment, practice merges in Practice, our life merges in a life of depth. A life based on the vast broadness of Emptiness rather than the mere smallness of this' and thats'.

So, before commitment we have a Prior Commitment which keeps things in perspective. Which allows us to commit ourselves to anything, to enter totally, without becoming lost. This Commitment allows us to work like a fanatic without being one; to give everything to a task while remaining clear and empty inside.

It's not so complicated! It's just being committed to the calmness of mind which is always there before agitation arises, to the stillness from which action arises, to the depth which always lies beneath the surface. It's commitment to the Emptiness of the Return.

And, actually, there's no other way. If we don't have this Prior Commitment, practice itself will delude us, and commitment itself will only confuse us as it will become inevitably bound up with gaining-mind.

Even though commitment seems out of fashion these days here's a kind of commitment which is not limiting, which makes things easier. This great Commitment of ours is like the buoyancy of water, or like gravity — you can't see it, but you can easily see and feel its effects.

We can skim along on the surface of life; we can enter the shallows; or, we can dive to the very depths. But, remember, to dive to the depths is not to go anywhere, it's to Return. The choice is always ours. At each moment the responsibility for a life of depth lies, not with our apparent outward situation, but only with ourselves.

Ironically, even a whole life of practice might still be a shallow one! That small concept of practice may never go beyond itself to become Practice; that small way may never go beyond itself to become Way. That small self may never come to know itself as Self.

A life of Practice however, is depth itself. It's not a way toward that depth. It is depth! Though this is hard to understand at first, still we have to begin by intuiting this simple truth: we have to see that practice is a way of going somewhere, while Practice is the way of Returning.

If we don't see this clearly we will have many difficulties regardless of the great efforts that we might be making. Even because of them. But if we do understand, then practice becomes Practice and we come to see that life is depth, beginningless, mysterious, depth just as it is.

CLARITY

Clarity Through Looking Clearly

The sage-like state of clarity begins with objectivity, impartiality. One of the old guys, S'eng T'san said that following the Way isn't all that difficult, you just have to avoid continually pitting one thing against the other, "this" against "that," and thereby fragmenting the world into opposites. So here's an exercise to sense "the undivided," to heal the world which we have managed to cleave apart.

Go through your musty closet of memories and pick one or two that particularly hurt to remember. You know, the mistakes, the embarrassments, the "I should'ves." Expose them to the light of clarity. Look impartially at these charged issues without flinching, without defending. Take them out, expose them to this powerful light until there's no charge left. Until you no longer cringe before them. Then look at your plans, look at anything where you have a stake in the outcome. Don't add, don't subtract, just look.

This is internal housekeeping, true, but also much more than that; it's learning to use your own innate clarity to Return ... to Clarity! To Return to the state of non-divisiveness with S'eng T'san and heal the world around you.

A LIFE OF CLARITY

If we're really intent about living a deeper life, a life of Practice, and hear about something called clarity — we *want* it! Same with enlightenment, even enlightening. We *want* them, to make things better, easier, more pleasant, whatever.

Well, we *think* that we want this thing called clarity, but what we *really* want is that state before wants of any kind at all arise. We want to be free of want!

We want to Return to the simplicity which preceded the divisive world of wants to begin with. So, we have to be careful! Careful so as not to engage our gaining-mind; careful to not make clarity just another acquisition.

To be able to look without being pushed and pulled by gaining-mind, bent out of shape by likes and dislikes *is* clarity. But just as there is practice and Practice, depth and Depth, there is also clarity and Clarity. So, while just being cool and calm, clear and neutral *is* important and *is* the way to clarity — it's not the whole show. Not at all.

For Clarity is all of that and yet something more — or less! Clarity is actually very simple. It's really just to cease identifying with the antics of the shallow mind. It's to reverse perspective, to calmly watch those antics without involvement. It's to be the blue sky through which all manner of cloud shapes course without changing its inherent spaciousness one whit.

So, though calmness is clarity, this reversal of perspective alone is Clarity. This is the only way to enter the state before wanting — paradoxically, of course, the state which we *really* want to begin with. Pressureless, desireless Clarity.

We have to move smoothly; we can't be too rough, too clumsy, or else we'll engage our gaining-mind and then everything will become confused. You have to be subtle, you have to *ease* into it. Don't just want not to want! Of course not.

Sometimes, of itself, the calmness of clarity will arise only to depart on its own. This is another difference between clarity and Clarity. The first arrives and departs with circumstances, it's not quite the real thing. But the second, Clarity, is not dependent on calming, or advantageous conditions — it's really there all the time just waiting to be noticed. It's the big blue sky. It's you. It's us. It's not being a cloud.

THE WAY OF ENQUIRY

For most, the purpose of questions is merely to get answers, but there is another kind of questioning which actually goes much deeper than that. So, although the Way of Enquiry might seem like a way of questions and answers, or even just asking a lot of questions, what we really mean by enquiry is a quite a bit different.

If we would understand the Way of Enquiry, a way of Practice, of Returning to Clarity, then we have to see that it is not merely a way of the intellect but rather a way to pierce *through* the surface tension of intellect, of thought.

The Way of Enquiry isn't difficult in the same way as breaking rocks, or digging ditches. Rather its difficulty lies in the need for subtlety, for acting without engaging the gaining-mind – and the gaining body too! You will understand just enough of this when you understand that it's more like using a scalpel, or shaving with a straight razor, than like using a hammer or a mattock. Even, constant, application is important.

Another thing about Enquiry – you can't rely on anyone else. Not on teachers, systems, books, even this one! You have to lean on enquiry, get stuck to it, get it in your hair, your eyes, your gut. Then hang out with it! And nobody else can do that for you. You just have to explore the territory for yourself.

So rather than merely asking a lot of questions, searching for a lot of answers, Enquiry is to enter into a primal question. A question which stops the mind, which reverses the continual outward flow of the mind. *That's* the whole point of enquiry.

You have to discover for yourself which questions have the potency to go beyond themselves — that have the power to go beyond their content to the very question mark, the primal question mark which stands at the end. You have to find questions which *begin* with a question mark rather than merely end with one. Questions which become only that primal question mark itself wordlessly glowing within. When you come to a question you can swallow whole, a question which becomes *physical* in nature, rather than merely intellectual — a question which pervades your whole body, even lightly, then you'll then know a little bit about enquiry.

The purpose of this wordless question is simply to reverse the outward stream of the mind. That *is* the answer. Clarity itself is the answer! Not another "word" answer, a "big head" answer. We have enough of those. It's the ultimate example of the saying, "ask a big question if you would get a big answer." A Big Question!

No one else can teach you to ask a question which fills the entire body. But that in itself is a pretty big hint. You like hints, don't you? Hints are good because they don't ruin everything. So here are a couple more: enquiry is "turning the light inward." Enquiry is an "implosion." See if you can *feel* it!

The mind is continually streaming outward, through the senses, through memory, through imagination, at the behest of gaining-mind. It's always running around shopping, accumulating. It's "consumer-mind." Picking and choosing, buying and rejecting, in relation to *everything* around us. It's really just the "world as shallows." Clarity? No way!

When we learn this simple, though subtle skill of reversing the outward flow of the mind through enquiry, we come to know a little bit about Clarity. And one thing we begin to see, which is really all we need to know about clarity, is that clarity is *not* the state where confusion never arises. It's the state which remains clear and undisturbed regardless whether confusion arises or not! This is very important!

What is a real question? A Big Question? Well, in "The Two-Edged Sword" we talked about the warrior-sages' search for the form of their past. That's a Big Question. It goes beyond itself. It's relevant to anyone. While, what a couple of old guys from another land said to each other a thousand years ago - well, maybe it is, maybe it isn't! Only you can tell if it's a question you can enter, one you can swallow. One which can swallow your consumer-mind.

Okay, the bottom line — what's the point, the real point of all this? Of a primal question with no answer?

The point is *meditation!* The answer is *meditation!* And not the kind that's merely a mental posture, another "consumerism." Not the kind you might try to learn from books, teachers, systems. *Real meditation.* The kind which is like a piece of paper folded back on itself. Nothing to get or gain that you don't already have.

TRUE FREEDOM

Whatever our practice, if we would understand it as Practice, as a Way, then we should really try to understand what freedom is. True Freedom.

Is freedom being able to do whatever you want? Many seem to think so, and there's no denying that personal and political freedom are very important. But, *then* what? Is that all there is?

Because if that's all there is to freedom, then even if no one oppresses us, even if we can do whatever we "want," we will still be quite limited! And we may still have no clue at all as to what true freedom really is.

Rather than being limited by others, if we're not careful we may be limited by *ourselves*. By us! More than that we may actually be *oppressed* by ourselves. In fact if we can't accurately determine just what true freedom is, we can say almost certainly that we *will* be oppressed.

How much of our day is spent mechanically, how much of our life? How much of our day, our life, is spent *reacting* to stimulation, rather than *responding*, our response emerging from clarity? How much time is spent in the long corridor of habit force? Do you get the drift? Is *that* freedom? Do we insist on seeing everything in terms of the past? Is *that* true freedom? No!

So, when we see that even if we somehow could have the capability to do whatever we want — *that what we want might be the problem* — then we come closer, much closer to the realm of freedom.

We have memory, desire, habit force, and these are all the extension of the past into the present. We have imagination, the extension of the past into the future. And, we have the Return. The unpressured, uncompulsive mind, the mind of clarity. The mind beyond the grip of the past. This is the mind through which all limitations of past thinking flow, and yet remains undisturbed. The mind in which something new, something fresh can happen. Fresh from the mind which is not simply "this" or "that." The mind which is not simply split into opposites.

The Buddhists end their *Heart Sutra* with something which roughly means, "Gone, gone, gone beyond...." That's *it!* That's our true freedom. But let's not begin by limiting *that* true freedom right away. You know, dragging it into the long hallway of habit, killing it, mounting it on the wall there. Dead, but with a plaque beneath that reads "True Freedom" or even "Gone beyond." Not being trapped by the small, or the big. Or even the Big! That's true freedom. That's "gone beyond." And it's not something you just acquire once and for all! It's *balance,* a continual process, you need to do it all your life! Don't kill it and mount it in the long hallway, labeled, hung there with all your other "treasures."

So, there's a kind of freedom wholly apart from just getting what you want, from being allowed to act unhindered from your habit force.

It's freedom to adapt, to adjust smoothly to obstacles. *Before* you collide with them! It's freedom to respond freshly, based on our clearest mind. It's both the freedom to be cool and calm *and* the freedom that arises *from* being cool and calm, too!

Well, once again, it's another chapter about the same thing! We have a hundred ways to say it around here! We call it the Return. Remember?

True freedom is the ability to ease back into the state before the world of opposites. And, opposites in themselves aren't *bad* – to think like that only creates more opposites. No, it's only when they distract us from the Return, from the Whence from which they came that opposites begin to cause way too many problems.

So, real freedom. Are you ready? Here goes: To view all opposites as related parts which oppose each other is the beginning. To see the essential sameness of opposites, the balanced state which we call the yin-yang is next. Finally, to allow opposites to remind you, and so Return you to the Source, the pool of no opposites, and then to act from *there*. That's true freedom! That's gone, gone beyond. Gone totally Beyond!

OPINIONS

Opinions are about opposites. About optical illusions. About opposition. Having opinions is "doing our part" to sustain the Sphere of the Rolling Mirror. Opinions help us to distort the original clarity and pure reflection of our mind and turn it into something like a carnival mirror. They are the cheap lenses through which we view this sphere and everything within it. Go ahead, have them if you must but don't *cherish* them. Because that's where the trouble starts....

Opinions are about opposites! They split the Rolling Mirror into pieces and hence split the mind which holds them too tightly. So, ease up! Let them be, but don't feed them. Just see them as mist, or dust. That's the way! Then they can't harm you.

It's a very graceful life, a very rare life, which can see the advantage of one thing without making it oppose all other things, which can walk North without downgrading all the remaining directions. A graceful life, a life based on clarity rather than the opposition of limited viewpoints.

So, to be able to Practice, to Return to Clarity, we continually try to take the bigger view. And the bigger view is to always be wary of opinions, always look at the smallness of their limited viewpoint. For where is clarity when they arise?

Do we really need strong opinions about anything? Do we need to judge others so as to avoid their mistakes? Do we really need to throw out "this" to grasp at "that"?

Because the Rolling Mirror becomes very small when we use our minds like this! We reduce the world to the size of a single thought. Then the world becomes too small to breathe deeply. You'll just feel cramped. And everyone around you will feel cramped too! Because opinions take up too much room while conversely making the world much too small!

So we don't judge others too much, we don't look too critically or too closely at their apparent faults. There's simply no time, no room for that. If we become caught by such limited views we split the Rolling Mirror into pieces. Bad luck! Our sense of wholeness is lost. And, all over *what?*

When we come to understand the Return a little bit more we begin to have its wholeness, its spaciousness, its clarity for a benchmark. A standard, but a standard based on the Return rather than the limited view of opinions. It's really Nothing. Emptiness. It's allowing the mind to be big and broad.

And when that happens we don't need to worry too much about opinions for they will have lost much of their power over us. Against the background of clarity they will somehow ring with a note of falsity, of shrill-ness, as soon as we voice them, even *think* of them. Then your opinions can't shrink your world. Or anyone else's.

Strongly held opinions become tempered, balanced, in the flame of clarity while weakly held views just arise and are consumed. Back to Emptiness! *Ahh!*

The most insidious carnival mirrors are our subtle opinions, our covert, remarkably elusive views of ourselves and the Rolling Mirror. To even *glimpse* these you have to be pretty sharp! Only the real, authentic, Blue Sky Mind can see them clearly. And that's good! That's what makes Practice continually interesting! Those subtle delusions are the only things that make a life of *enlightening* possible! How boring things would be otherwise! You don't want things to be boring do you?

So, it's "opinions are dead, long live opinions!" Just when you think they're gone, here they come again! That's the way it is. All you can do is let them live or die as they will while you just expose them to the light of clarity and watch. Don't feed them, don't cherish them. Just keep an eye on them. That's all.

Use clarity for your benchmark and things won't get out of hand. How long do you have to do that? For the rest of your life! So, be the clear blue sky and not just the cloudy sum of small views! Clouds, clouds, clouds ... ephemeral specks floating in the expanse.

THE GOOD FRIENDS

No one else can live a life of Practice for you. No one else can teach you that which you need to explore and discover for yourself. It's very important to understand this thoroughly at the very outset.

Yet, if we can begin with this understanding we may be ready to meet a Good Friend. Being ready to meet a Good Friend, we *might* actually recognize one when we do meet. That would be fortunate because Good Friends usually don't wear labels proclaiming who they really are. You have to be awake! Otherwise you'll be standing next to a Good Friend in a check-out line and be too preoccupied to notice. And, it's safe to say, that's already happened! So, assuming that you *are* ready, and actually *do* recognize a Good Friend when you meet — it's even rarer to have created the fortuitous circumstances in your life that will allow you to make use of your opportunity!

A Good Friend doesn't care how good of a job you have — that's what your parents are for! And a Good Friend isn't more likely to be your friend if you're beautiful, or any less likely if you're poor. Good Friends may not be too interested in your material success here in the Rolling Mirror, or how straight your teeth are, but they do care about you in very different ways. They care about your clarity (if *you* care about it!) and the quality of your action, and of your inaction, too. While your family, friends, lovers may be concerned with *what* you do — a Good Friend is more interested with *how* you do what you do. With the very depth and the Flow of your actions. They care about you in ways that people close to you may not even notice! And they care more if you Return, than if you return. So they'll never bind you.

A Good Friend will always simplify things. Yet, when you are unclear, confused, holding on to things, that "simplifying" can make things very complicated for you! You just have to view the Good Friend's actions from the vantage point of Clarity to appreciate their cleanness, spareness, their simplicity. And taking this vantage point often — just so you can figure out what your Good Friend is up to *now* — is, of course, one of the unusual benefits of having a Good Friend at all. You have to reverse perspective just to know what's going on!

Good Friends go through life without depending on any specific title or rank, *and they see others in the same way.* Because of this, they go through life open and ready to make a deep, unique relationship of Clarity with every person they meet, or even brush shoulders with! Though few ever notice. But that's no problem. Because they don't carry around set ideas of themselves, they're just as ready (and willing) to be ignored! But if you *do* notice, then a relationship, even for a moment, with a Good

Friend is like a sound investment — you'll always get a good return on everything you put in. And, a good Return too, if you watch closely and stay awake!

A Good Friend is a clearly reflecting mirror. Since their own wants are very minimal they reflect yours immediately, and with clarity. This makes some people uncomfortable, while it makes others feel like they're coming home.

Your Friend will be comfortable with change and Flow, sometimes exasperatingly so, and will see to it that you don't become attached to form, or emptiness, or even *Emptiness* for very long — let alone dogma, opinions, rigid views. Just when you think you've found a comfortable spot to hang out, your Good Friend stands up, stretches, and moves on. Then what do you do?

But they don't *want* anything from you! That's an important point. And they won't take what isn't freely given. If you want to stick around that's up to you; when you feel it's time to leave they won't stop you from going. A Good Friend takes care that you don't become too dependent. These are just some ways to tell who you're really with!

A Good Friend is not your boss! And doesn't want to be. They're not always preaching at you, telling you what to do! Rather they just enter totally into whatever they happen to be doing. They act totally and then they pause, without telling you what you've just witnessed. What you see is what you get! But it's up to you to drop your preoccupation with yourself long enough, and often enough, to see at all....

Because of this, and because your Good Friend isn't constantly telling you "what's going on," it's easy to forget. It's easy to forget and start to think that your Friend is doing *just what you're doing.* Becoming continually attached to appearances, to name and form. You know what happens.

So, watch it! If that's true, then see it clearly – but if not, Return from confusion. When you share a Return with a Good Friend, or *because* of a Good Friend, that's practice, that's clarity. But eventually, if you can just avoid taking things for granted, just sharing company with a Good Friend is Practice, Clarity in itself. You'll both just perform your actions naturally without calling unnecessary attention to them. You won't need labels. "Student." " Teacher." You'll change and flow together, go forth and Return together. The relationship itself becomes your Reminder. Then you'll hardly even need to say a word! Even about the Way, about Practice, about Clarity! Just two Good Friends rolling with the Mirror.

THE TURNAROUND

The Turnaround occurs when thinking becomes the secondary rather than the primary way in which we relate to the world. It does *not* mean that you stop thinking! But after the Turnaround you no longer accord thought quite the same importance as before. This is the point beyond which thought doesn't really bind you. The point where you finally allow the world to be what it really is.

It's not enlightenment – it's *better* than enlightenment! It's not a *finality,* rather a change of perspective. Most of all, it's not an *experience* but a threshold beyond which all experience is forever changed. When the turnaround occurs, we look the same, yet then we can say with Tennyson's Ulysses,

> I am a part of all that I have met;
> Yet all experience is an arch
> Wherethro' gleams that untravelled world
> Whose margin fades,
> Forever and Forever when I move.

Experience is no longer a separate thing which *happens* to us. Experience, the world, we, ourselves are emergences from Emptiness. For us this is not a theory but a fact. So thought, which arises from Emptiness but does not have the ability to do justice to its own Source, becomes relegated to a secondary role. The arising and disappearing of thought *is* its significance, rather than its particular *content*. Rather than its assigned meaning. It's a release of energy, a flash of lightning! That's a completely different way of looking at it, isn't it?

But you have to understand that this Turnaround is not a trophy, a goal, an acquisition. It's not a point to capture but a point beyond which perspective is reversed more often than it isn't. *Thought, beyond this point, is no longer the primary way in which you experience the world.* That's it. That's enough!

If you make a goal of it, though, you will just end up the servant of thought anyway, and your gaining-mind will keep you away from the Turnaround for a long time. So, as always, be careful how you begin!

There's no amount of practice that will bring you to the Turnaround. Only Practice will do! And it *is* difficult, but not so difficult as we like to make it.

You Return, but for a brief moment — it's like tasting the smallest crumb; it's hard to know just what you're eating! You open your eyes for the briefest instant — it's hard to know just what you're seeing! Would you like to go on a vacation for only a moment? Spend an instant at your destination and then return? Or would you like to hang out there for awhile, get to know your way around, discover the points of interest? Well, same with the

Return – you have to hang out there for awhile to get reacquainted with Nothing!

And, you do have to begin with a moment, an instant. But that's not going to be enough. You have to hang out, go deeper, learn your way around! Some say that an instant's enough for enlightenment. Plenty of time, right? But it's *not* enough for the Turnaround. And the Turnaround, remember, is better than enlightenment. Without the Turnaround with its reversed perspective, enlightenment can actually *mislead* us, make us very *pleased* with ourself! Uh-oh!

No, the Turnaround takes Practice. It occurs when we Return more and more often, and spend more and more time there. That's Practice. We go there so often there's a point where we recognize it as home. And not just our vacation home, either, but our main home. Then our perspective reverses. We can use thought without being used by it. Then experience just points the way home. Then we can come and go as we please, but still know where to Return.

The Turnaround is the point beyond which things get easier — *even when they're hard!* But it takes Practice. It takes acting from stillness. Most of all, it takes Returning. More and more often, for more and more time. Then things will turn around!

You can't "get" Clarity! And, you can't really "become" clear. If you truly understand this point, yet see no reason to give up, then Practice becomes less baffling, more clear.

Clarity is looking from the state before confusion arises, before opinions or compulsion arise. Paradoxically, Clarity is being able to watch confusion, opinions, compulsion, from the state before any of them arise! Once again, the logical mind hears this and immediately becomes confused! Well, let it! For within the vast blue skies of Clarity, those are just clouds floating on through, borne on the winds of change.

The blue sky is independent of the billowing clouds, and this prior, clear mind, this Blue Sky Mind, doesn't get confused — even when the clouds of confusion are present! And even if our logical mind has a problem with this (along with a lot of other things!), we still have to Return in order to understand.

Clarity. We just Return over and over to this calm, unpressured Blue Sky Mind. We begin to see that it's always there even when apparently obscured by passing clouds. That's our Way, whatever our practice may be.

So don't try to "get" it. And don't try to "become" a Returner or the clouds pile up thicker and deeper. Just Return to that ever-present blue sky and see what you see! Don't add. Don't subtract. Don't edit. Is that clear?

FLOW

Discover Non-Action

The old guys talked about non-action, yet non-action is a still a way of acting. They called it "wu-wei," and it's a real secret of putting these principles to use. Wu-wei is to act naturally, without excess tension, without compulsion. It's the way to do things in accord with the Way!

There are two parts to this exercise. First, STOP! That's right, stop doing anything! Pause. Pause until every trace of impatience dissolves. A moment, a hundred moments — whatever it takes. Become aware of that energy normally squandered through speediness, impatience, a furrowed brow. Pause, and do nothing as this energy accumulates in a smooth, flowing current, emerges like a clear spring.

Then, emerge with it, lightly, smoothly, and do a task. Pick something smooth, rhythmic. Polish a mirror, sweep a floor, do the dishes. Don't be compulsive. Be like a blue sky. Take care of this smooth flow of emerging energy. In the beginning carry it like precious crystal, not too lightly, not too tightly. This is non-acting — the best way to do things. Everything! Familiarize yourself with it. It's drawing water, carrying wood, like our old friend P'ang Y'un.

A LIFE OF FLOW

When we think of "beauty" associated with human beings, most people think of physical beauty. But what is even more beautiful is someone living a life of Flow. Whatever their physical appearance might be! This is real beauty, a rare kind of beauty which few seem to attain. This is beauty beyond appearances.

In various types of movement we occasionally see this waterlike flow, in skiing, in ice skating, in martial arts, but very seldom do we see it in the greater movement of life. Why? Because we're patterning organisms! We tend to fall into patterns and remain there until evicted. And it's much easier for patterning organisms like us to recognize and adapt to the relatively few (and more predictable) changes required by movement, by sport, than to the exponentially greater possibilities (and unpredictability) of the Big Changer. To the infinite number of moving, changing possibilities within the Rolling Mirror.

But that's what a life of Flow takes! It's being water, being a stream adapting to a constantly shifting bank and a constantly changing bed. If we hold onto things, spend too much time in the past, become nothing more than a patterning organism, we'll lose the Flow. We'll lose it because we can't adapt soon enough. No grace.

To live a life of Flow is a beautiful thing, more beautiful than merely looking beautiful — but it's very rare. It's rare due to confusion. It's rare due to not being ready. It's rare because the mind isn't lubricated, things don't flow on through smoothly.

In a little known practice they recite:

> May my mind be clear.
> May I live fearlessly in the
> Mind of Readiness.
> May I rely on nothing but Emptiness.

That's the way to Flow! But if you had to, you could just reduce it to, "May I rely on Nothing."

TRUST IN THE FLOW

Some people like to talk about emptiness. But the emptiness they usually dredge up is just some kind of *invisible* emptiness, an *intangible* emptiness. Maybe that's why they call it emptiness — because they can't find it anywhere! Or maybe it's like microbes — you can't see them but you know they're there anyway!

But our emptiness is quite different. It's not just invisible, intangible — it's not just the opposite of form. No! It's emptiness but sometimes we have to call it *form* because they aren't really separate things. The logical mind may or may not have a problem with this, but it's all just a matter of perspective. Just remember — our emptiness isn't just some invisible, intangible fantasy, in fact, you can't go *anywhere* without seeing it!

When our emptiness starts moving, changing, we sometimes call if flow. But when we open our eyes wide and begin to bump into this flow everywhere, begin to recognize it anywhere we go — when it starts to become recognizable as a thread which runs through all existence, then we call it Flow. And it's this Flow we're interested in. *But it doesn't matter what you call it!* Flow is Emptiness. And, as a way of Practice, to "rely on Nothing," to "rely on nothing but Emptiness," is to rely on the Flow. It means rolling with the Mirror, befriending the Big Changer. But it takes trust....

A life of Practice can become very difficult without trust in the Flow. You may understand everything else there is to know, have a lot of self-discipline, have a strong connection with the Way, but it won't be enough. We're patterning organisms! If we don't know the secret of letting a creative spark, an open space, into our lives, our Practice will be reduced to practice, a dead thing with no vitality of its own. Without this living quality, this vitality, we may feel as though we're *trudging*. And it's not the kind of "hard training" that helps us to grow — it's the kind that just makes us weary.

To make this dead thing come alive, to transform practice into Practice, whether for the first time or the thousandth, we have to trust in the Flow. Trusting in the Flow, relying on Nothing, doesn't mean that we just find some new thing to attach to, a new idea to depend on. And, it doesn't mean that we cease taking responsibility for our actions. Not at all!

It's simply like being in water; it's very tiring, there's lots of thrashing around until you come to trust in the fact that the water will support you. In its *buoyancy*. Trust in the Flow doesn't mean that you stop swimming! It means that you become conscious of more than just the effort of moving your arms and legs — it means that you become conscious of the wonderful feeling of buoyancy *while* you're swimming. Trust in the Flow. It's refreshing!

Don't make the mistake of thinking that the main

difference between practice and Practice, flow and Flow, is just one of energy, of becoming more tired one way than the other. No! The real difference is this: the end of long practice often comes to mean that you rely on nothing. It's a way of inner strength, yet one that can't go beyond itself. If you're not very careful, you become more and more important the longer you practice! *The mind hardens with experience.* But the way of Practice is different, it's simply to rely on Nothing. And Nothing, Emptiness, is Flow! This trust is what transforms life into the Way. It's not just staying afloat, *it's being buoyant!*

It's a kind of confidence, maybe, but it's *not* positive thinking. It's that quality which allows you to not think! It's the only thing which allows you to trust in the infinite possibilities beyond thought. In "no-mind."

In the martial arts it's simple. You stand before your attackers and you don't think about what they're going to do, or about what *you're* going to do. You trust in the Flow and then your prior training will manifest in the clearest way. The Clearest Way. In life it takes this same emptiness, this same trust, but for some reason it's much more difficult. Why? Because the Big Changer doesn't announce who the attackers really are. No labels. No "get ready, here it comes." It takes real trust in the Flow, in Emptiness to relax and be open, let the mind soften, forget about yourself, and yet be ready. But that's what it takes! And, actually, in martial arts too, we're always looking to Return to this even bigger, softer mind required in life. Then we are more ready for the un-announced, unlabeled attack, which may or may not even be a person, an attacker! It may be a situation. It may be spontaneity having a bit of sport with us!

The pitfall? The usual. Gaining-mind in one of its many disguises. Gaining-mind smiling, agreeing, saying, "I'll trust in Flow, but here's the deal...." So watch it! Don't try to trust in the Flow so you can get everything you want. That's not it.

No, trust in the Flow doesn't mean that you'll always get what you want. (Unless of course you want what you get!) Rather it's to soften your mind, give you the ability to flow with the Flow. To roll with the Mirror. To not say "uh-oh" when the Big Changer shows up at your place uninvited.

It's to be *buoyant* in the mysterious, silent, continual stream of the Flow. It's to adjust smoothly, easily to change. It's to become less, rather than more important. That's all.

CHANGE AND FLOW

Change is the constant. Change is the Way of all things. And the Way for human beings involves adjustment. Harmonizing with the continual change of all things — and each other! The Way for human beings then is simply to Return, to become a part of the Way of all things! Why exclude yourself?

We talked about trust in the Flow. That's when we stop thrashing around in the flowing water of the Way. That's when we allow the perception of change, of *all* changes, to move unhindered through the deep stillness of our minds. Coming. Going. Gone! Don't hold on! Because if you do, the mind will be disturbed, the sense of flow interrupted, the Way, lost.

So, don't hold on! This actually is a great secret of the martial arts, all of them. Allow the perception of your attackers to move through the stillness of your mind. Don't sacrifice that stillness — act from it! Unfortunately, even those who can do this in the martial arts, in movement, in sports, seldom rest in this deep, still mind while in the greater movement of life. This is too bad, because even if we become proficient, even excellent, in only this very limited way, it isn't enough. We'll be estranged from the Way. From Practice. There might be flow at certain times, at certain places, but not Flow.

Whatever our practice, it doesn't have to be martial arts, it could be anything, or nothing – we should stick close to this and see if we can discover this still mind through which changes flow. Blue Sky Mind. Immovable mind. It doesn't matter what you call it or where you heard about it!

Paradoxically (as usual!), this still deep mind is capable of keeping up with quick changes and responding faster than the mind which is always moving around. Trust in the Flow is trusting that this immovable mind is enough, that it will allow us to flow with all situations, easily, and smoothly, with a minimum of friction. The old guy Chuang-tzu said,

> In motion like water
> In stillness like a mirror
> Respond like an echo
> Be subtle as though disappearing.

That's it! That's trust in the Flow, immovable mind, all the rest of it, too. But how can we discover this immovable mind – this still, deep mind that is undisturbed by changes? By trying to be calm all the time? No way!

The only way to enter immovable mind, Blue Sky Mind, is by *watching.* That's right, by watching the passing stream. That's *"in stillness like a mirror."* But you can't edit, can't add or subtract. You can't hope against hope! You'll just be *"subtle as though disappearing."* That means the "you" who sticks fingers in all the pies, the "you" who is puzzled by flow, steps back, becomes subtle, and stops interfering. Watch the passing stream like *that,* and there it is – Blue Sky Mind.

And though we sometimes call it the Immovable, or motionless mind, it's not *rigid!* Though you understand that now as you read, in practice, in long, ongoing day-in, day-out practice you'll forget. And when you forget and get immovable mind mixed up with rigidity, then you'll look foolish to those around you. Even if they're not sure why – you will! And they'll be right, because it'll be the difference between posture and *posturing!*

So, even though the mind is immovable it's actually quite soft and open. *But watchful without trying.* Another paradox! You have to make the jump between intellectual understanding of change and the actual awareness of change as it happens.

It's the only way to consistently roll with the Mirror, to *be* "in motion like water, in stillness like a mirror." It's not just for martial artists. No way! It's how to live a life of Flow. And, like riding on the crest of a wave, we do it best when we're not thrashing around!

SELF-ESTEEM

This one, like commitment, is a little tough for most people to get down. But it *is* important, very important, so give it your best shot. If you *can* understand it, if you can even *read* about it without getting too excited, agreeing, disagreeing, then you're probably ready to live a life of Flow. Even if you don't get anything else!

But remember, all this isn't about some new pop-psychology, or about how everyone should feel good about themselves whatever they do, or about cultivating warm and cuddly feelings. It's about the Way! It's about living a life of Practice. It's *not* about finding new ways to think about thinking and feel about feeling.

Most people today are searching for self-esteem. For ways to feel good about themselves, about the small "who" of "who they are." But rather than self-esteem, which doesn't go beyond itself, we just esteem the Self. There's another difference between practice and Practice for you.

Instead of esteeming this jumbled, often confused collection of thoughts and experiences, Practice begins when you begin to esteem the Life Force which is you, the Blue Sky Mind, which is really you too. The Life Force instead of habits, the Blue Sky Mind instead of changing clouds. Esteeming the Self. It's really just the same commitment to the prior, Clear Mind that we talked about before.

Because if we don't understand this point, Practice becomes just another appropriation of gaining-mind, another product to buy, something to make you feel good about yourself. And Practice is a very different thing entirely. Practice is the way of "gone, gone, gone beyond." It's the way of exploring the vast realm beyond thought and memory, *then* coming back to this world of cars and trains and practicing what you learned. Patiently and persistently. So, we can't make a clean start from trying to become better, from trying to become "perfect," from trying to become a "master." From trying in any way to build self-esteem. But if you want to enter in a heartbeat, to go beyond all these words in an instant, you just have to reverse perspective. Esteem the Self which includes your little self. The Blue Sky through which your little cloud blows around.

Though there can't be any "getting," any "bettering," you know, gaining-mind, there is *something*. This *something* comes from esteeming the Self. It's a purification, a simplifying, a learning that comes entirely from the silent, but powerful influence of the benchmark. It's like bathing in the Blue Sky Mind (which you're really doing anyway!) and becoming refreshed. It's the way which you can enter, only in the complete absence of compulsion, of gaining-mind.

The doorway to this big Self-esteem is very easy to find. It's *gratitude.* Not just towards this thing or that, not

just for getting what you want. It's gratitude uncon-
nected with results! It's a different gratitude which lightly
fills your whole body. It's Returning to Clarity, to the
Self, nestling into the Life Force because that's who you
are — *not* for what you'll get. This gratitude is a very easy
way in but you can't be heavy handed about it. You have
to be subtle ("subtle as though disappearing"), so as not
to wake up gaining-mind who's fallen asleep while
guarding the door.

And regardless of all the seminars which offer quick
fixes, this works better, and faster. And it's free! You can
do it anywhere, anytime.

So, more self-esteem, or esteem the Self? It's up to
you. There's a way to not take yourself too seriously yet
still enter totally into everything you do. Gratitude's the
doorway. It's "gone beyond." And it's not so hard to
swallow if your mouth happens to be closed....

DOING WITHOUT DOING

A common criticism of the Way, of Practice, among those who really know nothing about it, is that there's simply no *time* for it! They don't know about *you* but *they* have things to *do!* You know that one. If not, you will.

They don't have time to flow because they're *busy people*. They don't have time to live a life of depth. In fact, they don't even have time to have time!

Actually, you have more in common than you might think. *Because they don't have time to waste and neither do you!* They don't have time to Practice, you don't have time to *forget* about Practice. And you both, meanwhile, *do* have things which need to get done. But, how? In what way?

How can you live a life of Flow, a way which seems to imply non-effort, yet still get things done? How can we do things so that they embody the deep, mysterious action of the Flow without becoming distracted by the task itself, by results themselves, by the compulsion to get one thing out of the way (out of the Way!) and immediately begin the next? Important questions!

For us, it's not enough to simply get things done. *How* we get things done; the quality of our action is important! Very important. The deep quality of our inaction too. When our action emerges cleanly from stillness our doing is no longer simply *doing* but rather the wonderful

91

and deep activity of the Flow. And, things still get done!

Are there any hints to help us get things done without becoming lost in the process? Hints which might help us to not interfere with the Flow? To do without becoming caught up in the *doing?* Because this is *practical* stuff, and it's one thing to talk about the Way and a very different thing to allow the Way to Flow through our actions. And besides, we like hints.

All formal ways, including the martial arts, calligraphy and flower arrangement, seem at first glance to be ways of getting things done; but what they really are, are ways beyond just getting things done. In other words, the *way* in which you get things done is the point. The Way in which you get things done. In all formal ways you are given a task to do and then asked to go beyond thought, become the action itself! All formal ways are ultimately about the Way. About letting the Flow act through you unhindered. *But so is everything else!*

For us, everything has to be like that. Everything we do is a way, though maybe not a formal way. This is really the only way to really learn about entering totally, about Flow, about trust in the Flow. And it's the only way even if you study many formal ways! Some like to say:

> May my mind be clear
> May I live fearlessly
> In the mind of Readiness
> May I rely on nothing but Emptiness.

Remember? Well, that's the way of the Way. That's the way to do anything. The way to do beyond doing! Anything — even cooking! It's not just for the martial arts. Not at all. If you can swallow that whole, fine. But if you feel like you need a little chewing first, then here are a few points that may help:

There's no such thing as purely mental or physical action. In our life of Practice we are always studying how to balance our minds and bodies. If we would "meditate" we begin by adjusting our posture; if we would face an attacker we begin by emptying our minds. The same goes for mathematics, and cooking, or carving. So, begin well.

We have to discover Pure Intent, the way to direct the mind and body without causing a reaction. It's the only way to have intention without excess tension. It's the way to do a task so that the will does not oppose the Flow. You have to learn this one on your own — you have to do less to do more. You begin by allowing all the extra things you've learned from gaining-mind to fall away and proceed from there. It's the way of action from stillness. Pure Intent.

The Way of Flow is like any other balance discipline. Everything works best from a neutral, centered position. It's how to punch, how to dig, how to chop vegetables, or write a letter. It's the way we move in martial arts, or on the street. It's like skiing, but skiing life. And it's not just a physical thing, it's a mentally neutral and centered position too. But don't create a hardened little point in your mind or body and call that "center." Just don't lean mentally or physically, and you'll begin to understand on your own.

So, there's a few hints. Start by becoming aware of *how* you do things. Learn to do things smoothly without excess friction, or slippage. Experiment, flow. No one can teach you these things, but they're not that hard to learn. Just don't lean. Don't hurry. And, don't drag your feet. Do things like you have all the time in the world, yet none to waste!

ROLLING WITH THE MIRROR

When the old guys talked about the Way they often spoke of water. Water and its seemingly endless capacity for adjustment, for seeking the way through, for flowing around obstacles. In the Rolling Mirror, our world, we can be like smoothly flowing water, or we can be the slightest bit late, the slightest bit out of position, out of harmony with the Big Changer. Then the Flow is lost.

So, rolling with the Mirror is our way of Flow and, ultimately, our "wayless way" of Practice. It's to Flow with change. With one type of attitude when the mind is hard, it's very difficult; while with another type of attitude, the one which we must discover, we can't help but to live smoothly, flow with change, roll with the continually Rolling Mirror.

When the mind is right, everything is right. Then we accompany all events without strain. We surf on the crest of events. But, paradoxically this doesn't mean that we become limp, ineffectual; that we try to yield ourselves to death! It means that we have a bright yet soft, alert yet open mind which is not continually trying to escape.

That's how we accompany events. When there's no hint of escape. And when we accompany events without trying to escape, there's no strain. Then we are like a good driver, we can accelerate, brake, change gears, steer, but we *can't* shut our eyes, or turn our heads away from the road. So, rolling with the Mirror, flowing with Flow, is more than just a feeble acceptance of whatever happens, it's being in tune with what's happening, not fighting it; responding rather than reacting.

If we try to escape, opposing our situation, tensing against it, we lose some very important things. *Timing. Rhythm.* And even if we do adjust without them we may do it at the wrong time. So, beyond *what* we do there's *how* we do. And beyond that is *when* we do. We may walk across a street with grace, balance, good posture, neither hurrying nor lagging, but if we do it at the wrong *time....*

Just as we see that there's practice and Practice, flow and Flow, clarity and Clarity – there's timing and there's big Timing too. Small timing is for getting out of the way, for not getting hit. It's for knowing when to speak and when to be quiet. It's useful, it's important, and it's hard to do anything really well without it.

Big Timing is something more. It includes the balancing of action and stillness, of tension and slackness, of concentration and diffusion, but even *more*, big Timing is the ability to move lightly from one situation to the next, using the stored energy of each situation to catapult into the next. And you have to be ready and open, "on," to sense just when that peak of energy will occur. Because once this point is reached, the stored energies of each situation enter the "decline phase" of their natural development. Then, instead of lightly skipping through life, dancing, you can only plod because you'll have nothing to work with.

To use *this* Timing, the Timing of Flow, requires "letting go," being able to let go of each situation as it peaks rather than as it begins to decay, as each must eventually do. This requires trust in the Flow, and the prior commitment to Nothing.

But it's *not* a way of evading commitments, of simply quitting when things get tough. It's a way, rather, of attunement, of adding fresh energies as called for to refresh and renew an "old" situation when possible. And when not possible, it's being attuned to the dissolution of the very forces which allowed the situation to come to be in the first place. It takes Clarity to see and act on this appropriately. So, it's not just *what* you do — but *how* and *when.* It's not something you can understand quickly. It's "skiing life," and, like skiing, it takes plenty of mileage to get the feel. You have to start with timing first, with flow and work up.

When we discover that attunement to the building and declining of forces, we come to sense the Timing which allows us to harmonize with those forces. Many people when they think of "harmony" somehow conjure up a world with no challenges, no surprises. But creating harmony is always a challenge; a challenge to our status quo. The Rolling Mirror continues to roll, the Big Changer drops in unexpectedly, and we don't want to get caught flat-footed.

So, rolling with the Mirror is our Way of Practice,

our Way to Flow. But it's not acceptance of whatever is happening, it's the acceptance of whatever has happened. A big difference.

It's a fluid process of adjustment which becomes possible when you don't try to escape. It takes timing usually, and Timing always. It's really just the study of current events — very current events. Not just the current events happening in far-off places, but the very current events happening right now, all around you, and in you too!

A Life of Flow. One of the most beautiful things — and one of the rarest. A human life like a mountain stream....

Well, it's quite easy to talk about flowing with the Big Changer, about harmony, about rolling with the Mirror, but the truth is, it's easy to get stuck in a pattern, a pattern where we expect things to conform to us much too much.

To be ready, poised. To sit as though ready to stand, to move as though ready to change direction. To turn off the automatic pilot and open your eyes. To be alive.

To move lightly and easily with life and yet to remain deep and silent inwardly is to live a life of Flow. It's the easiest way to go, the mountain stream way of doing things; and it's really just Practice in action.

WONDER

What Do I Really Know?

Mystery and Wonder are intertwined. What we think we know becomes devoid of wonder, and a life without wonder soon becomes devoid of richness, depth, of the Way itself....

This exercise is a return, through enquiry, to the wonder of not-knowing. Not-knowing is unlimited; knowledge is limited. Not-knowing is the ground of mystery, the land of wonder; a haven to be visited daily. It is the source of creativity, inventiveness, and tranquility all in one. Not-knowing is the only place from which freshness can emerge.

Of all the knowledge which you consider "yours," how much is merely the leavings, the transfusions of others? What have you truly learned on your own, through observation, intuition, enquiry? Return to not-knowing! Rest there awhile. Expect nothing. Then emerge gently to view the world with fresh eyes.

Not-knowing. Go there daily! This is meditation, rejuvenation, the source of creativity, even therapy, all rolled into one.

A LIFE OF WONDER

We live in this mysterious world as if we *understand* it and so wonder becomes lost. We live as if we know more than we don't know and that isn't true. It's only the predominance of the superficial mind that lets this occur.

Yet the mind of depth, the mind which perceives the forgotten spaciousness in and of the world of opposites, is a mind which understands the limits of this kind of superficial knowledge. And when you understand the enormity of what you *don't* know, and the mysterious, undefined spaciousness which then arises, you come to know something beyond merely knowing *things* — you come to know the Mind of Wonder. You come to know not-knowing!

Each moment of our lives we stand at a crossroads: We can reduce the profound to the mundane or we can intuit the continuous and vital mystery through which we move. We have a choice!

And it doesn't mean that we cease knowing things! But it does mean that we continually perceive the limits of that kind of knowledge That's all! It means that we perceive the enormity of not-knowing as well as the useful, but superficial world of intellectual knowledge. Then, intellectual knowledge remains as a tool instead of a barrier.

This not-knowing will allow the Rolling Mirror to return to what it really is. This alone will release the mind into the Mind of Wonder.

THE SOUNDLESS SOUND

Soundless sound? Our logical mind, the old mind of clouds, tells us that there can't be a soundless sound yet our intuitive nature has no problem with this at all.

But no matter how hard we listen we won't hear this soundless sound, this *pre-sound,* unless we discover another way to listen, a way to listen which lies not at the end of our ears but at the beginning of all of our senses. If you call it a sound, a vibration, a piece of mental phenomena, even the OM, it will be quite easy to go astray, to get lost in the shape of a new cloud with a new name.

The soundless sound, however, is not the notes but rather the intervals; not thoughts, but the spaces between thoughts! Yet our logical mind which wants to turn everything into a linear proposition, likes to make those intervals, those spaces, into a mere blankness alternating with notes, with thought. But you can't come to the soundless sound like that. Never.

You come to the soundless sound as soon as you see that that interval is not merely a small space between notes but rather the space which surrounds the notes, the space in which the notes occur. You come to the soundless sound when you realize this same truth about thought. To come to the soundless sound is neither to eliminate thought nor cherish it. Instead it's to come to the Emptiness which is not merely *between* each thought but which totally surrounds it! It is to come to the ocean which lies not merely between fish but all around them.

Our logical mind may have a problem in noticing this and our gaining-mind won't see it at all! Our gaining-mind sees the usefulness of the spaces between dominoes but easily forgets about the space surrounding those spaces!

Of course, once again, it's the same Blue Sky Mind which surrounds the clouds, the Blue Sky Mind which *includes* the clouds. The Blue Sky Mind which really is not separate from the clouds at all. There, we said it! But, if you want to really see this for yourself, you have to know the Blue Sky first so as not to become lost in cloud shapes. See the sky, you see the clouds too; but if you forget and concentrate too hard on the clouds, the clarity of the Blue Sky will disappear for you! Oh, it's true it won't be gone, but for you it might as well be. It's all just a matter of perspective.

So, to know the Blue Sky of your mind is to know the soundless sound. It's to become aware of the Emptiness through which thought arises, flows, and vanishes.

And to come to this soundless sound is to discover your inner teacher. Many people look for an inner teacher who talks, teaches in words, gives advice. Most of them, look for, and often find, an "inner teacher" who merely agrees with what they want to do anyway! Kind of a rubber stamp from out of the void. But this kind of "teacher" is just karma, just clouds.

The inner teacher that you really have, however, the teacher of the soundless sound is mute! Doesn't teach in words and concepts. No Way. *This* teacher is rather the emptiness through which your desire swims. This teacher is the light of your own mind. The Blue Sky. The soundless sound of your mind before attachment arises. A breakthrough – wisdom without words!

The way of listening to the soundless sound doesn't involve listening to any kind of mental phenomena, clouds, at all. Instead it's to listen and make a rapport with that clear Interior Void which you may have forgotten while you focused on things and shapes. While you may have become lost in the clouds.

We call it listening but really it's that *receiving* that we spoke of earlier. *Receiving* instead of incessantly transmitting all the time. Quiet!

So, a hint? Sure. Listen to a sound, anything at all. Follow the pathway of hearing back to the reservoir where all your senses merge. Back to where all your senses are still undivided. Go back to the sound of pre-sound. To the unpressured state. Listen to the soundless sound of waves lapping on the shore of the "pool-of-no-opposites." Return to the Blue Sky. Then know opposites, thoughts, clouds, in light of that listening. In the light of the teaching of the soundless sound.

BEING ALONE

Everyone in the Rolling Mirror, at times, has to be alone. How you spend that time is a very important question for anyone who would live a life of Practice. It is the depth and quality of that time alone which may determine the depth and quality of all the rest of your time, just as the depth and quality of your stillness can determine the power and grace of your subsequent actions.

To be alone well, without loneliness, is Practice, and emerging from that stillness into the company of others is also Practice. But the quality of that stillness, of that aloneness is important. Very important. Are you alone with a chattering mind focused on cloud shapes? If so, you're not really alone, even if you're the only one on an isolated mountain top, or an uncharted desert island. The pure quality of your aloneness hasn't blossomed, and the burdens of your past and future, poor company, keep you from Returning. Ironically, even loneliness can visit like an unwelcome guest and destroy your solitude!

Yet, as a person of Practice, when you're able to take a brief vacation from responding to the needs and energy of others, you should use your time well.

This means that, even for a short time, we ease back into the ever-present, unsupported, independent Blue

Sky Mind and remain there awhile. *That's* being alone, regardless of where we are! We don't just become "aware" of this mind — that's still really small. We Return, we *ease* back into it. We become like a folded sheet of paper. That's being alone, but even more, that's *meditation*.

It's not mysticism either, mysticism is being in love with experience. Massive, radical experience maybe but still experience. Really big, really beautiful clouds, even rainbows. *But it's not being alone.* Because it's not Returning. It's not Returning to the clarity of the Blue Sky which is there before, and surrounding, the awesome clouds of mysticism. Or the even the much bigger clouds of gaining-mind!

Being alone well, without loneliness, is "in stillness like a mirror." It's an opportunity to Return to the Blue Sky and listen to the soundless sound for awhile. It's an opportunity to learn from Nature without the distractions of others, of *doing,* of the one who just got left alone. Use your time well. It's a vacation. It's refreshing. But more than that, it's being the Blue Sky so that when you act, when you're in the thick of things again, there's a different basis for your actions. Your actions emerge from stillness like they should.

So, being alone is sometimes the easiest way to ease back into focus, to Return. But being with people is often the best way to Practice, expressing that clear stillness in action. Otherwise, what good is it?

In order to Practice, being alone shouldn't be an

escape. A vacation maybe. In order to Practice, being with people shouldn't be a craving. So, it's another "balance sport." Another way to Practice whether you have a formal practice or not.

And, sometimes you'll be lonely. You will. But that's a sign. A sign telling you to Return. Loneliness is natural, like a cloud. Sometimes it's even possible to feel lonelier in a crowd than alone. Still you should ask yourself if you're lonely because of isolation from people, or because you're isolated from your Blue Sky Mind? What do you say?

PRIORITIES OF WONDER

If you would live a life of Practice, a life of wonder, you have to examine your priorities. Because the wrong emphasis will reduce your Practice to just practice and your life of wonder to mere words.

You should look and see if you've created a paradox where you would live a life of wonder while retaining the same old way of looking at things, doing things, knowing things. You should especially look to see if you might be trying to take the vast mystery of Emptiness into the small room of your world as an ornament. It won't fit!

Establishing priorities is the prerequisite of Practice. That means to understand the relationship of clouds and sky, of action and stillness, of principle and technique. It means that as a farmer you don't make the mistake of thinking that the crops are more important than the soil; that as a grower you don't take care of the fruit and ignore the tree; as a breeder you don't neglect the mare to take care of the foal. It's just knowing what's important!

With good soil there will be more crops even if you have the odd bad year due to drought. With a healthy tree, more fruit to come. With a strong mare, more foals on the way. So, first things first, *take care of the source.* Of course, you'll take of the yield too, but to do things in the best way, that comes second.

And that's just how we Practice too! In fact, that's the only way that we can live a life of wonder. For us, the way to keep track of the clouds is to watch the sky. The way to know things is to begin with not-knowing! The way to really act well is to act from out of stillness. And though that may be contrary to everything you see people doing around you, it's just a question of priorities.

We can't make wonder arise. We can't live a life of wonder by trying. That's fact. Yet, when we don't neglect the soil of Emptiness, when we watch the sky to see the clouds, when our limited pieces of knowledge are seen floating within the vastness of not-knowing, *wonder is there!* It's not a word, it's not contrived. We simply live with a sense of the mystery of existence. We can't help it! When we don't neglect the source, when we act from out of stillness we get the same deep and mysterious feeling as when we see a flower bursting forth from the Void, or see a flash of lightning suddenly blazing forth from Emptiness. We participate in that!

The old guy Lao-tzu said that the Tao was like an empty vessel which can never be depleted. That's what we're talking about. Getting your priorities straight. He also said use it and you can't exhaust it. That's important too. But everyone does that. Our priority, in order to Practice, is to first remember the empty vessel. *That's* establishing priorities.

It's not belief. It's not dogma. It's a simple, clean, clear faith in the healthy soil. In the Blue Sky. In the vessel that can't be depleted. It's performing the smallest act with reverence. It's living in, and with, wonder. It's remembering what's important. So, first things first. Right?

NOT-KNOWING

When we lose our sense of wonder in life it's a sign that we know too much! It's true. Wonder is always the first casualty of too much knowing, while it always thrives in the rich soil of not-knowing.

Unfortunately, most people, when they suddenly realize that their lives have become dull, flat, devoid of wonder, look for answers. More knowing! This approach is like using gasoline to put out a blaze.

It's *questions* that are important here, not more answers. Not more pieces of knowledge. And not just any question either, but a real question which can reverse the habitual outward flow of the mind long enough to see. A question with the power to Return you to the vastness of not-knowing. *That's* where you'll find your wonder and nowhere else.

To learn to question in this manner is the way of Enquiry. It's the art of self-rescue and it's purpose is to keep you from drowning in the debris of knowing too much. Or just thinking that you do! Too much knowing obscures the mind. Destroys the sense of wonder. Replaces reverence with a shallow, affected, piousness. And, of course, not-knowing is the only natural remedy for this disease which swings wildly back and forth between terminal boredom and terminal distraction.

If you're a "knower," even enlightenment won't help you. Only not-knowing will do. Only enlightening, continually seeing how little you really know will do. Only that knowledge leads to real knowledge, big knowledge. The knowledge of not-knowing, the *knowledge of wonder*.

Sometimes you *have* to know things, it's true! How to get from "Hay" to "Bee." How to cook things. Fix things. Even fix things you cook! What then?

Just hold your knowledge lightly, keep your mind open and ready to flow. Keep your mind flexible instead of hard. That kind of knowing is the best way to know things. It won't interfere at all. That kind of knowing is using the mind skillfully and it won't harm your sense of wonder.

But sometimes you *really* need to know something and don't. What then? Turn your mind to the task, turn your mind to the question, frame it lightly. Then, Return, go back to Blue Sky Mind. That's right, go to not-knowing for your answer! That's the Way of Practice.

And, if you Return to the Blue Sky repeatedly and don't get your answer? Look! That *is* your answer!

LEARNING FROM NATURE

While it's true that there's a lot to learn *about* Nature, for us, as students of the Way – whatever our particular way – there's even more to learn *from* Nature. If we can temper our enthusiasm for accumulating ideas we can begin to assimilate a different sort of knowledge. A knowledge which is not only *about* things but a guiding force which helps us to do anything in the most correct way. Even Returning.

We come to this unique sort of knowledge through attunement to Nature, and the Mind of Wonder is both prerequisite and symptom of that attunement. And there's no substitute for it – nothing else will do! The Mind of Wonder is simply the open, empty cup which is ready to become filled!

Ecological issues have become very important these days as more and more people begin to recognize how critical these issues are to the health of our planet and everything on it, including ourselves. This is wonderful and extremely important, *yet it is not enough*. Because if we're not careful we may lose our attunement with the planet even as we try to help. We may become little more than insensitive missionaries committed to "helping" but with little rapport with the culture that we are trying to help. The danger of this is that even when we do make the "correct" action we may do it in such a way that can't possibly lead to lasting results. So, what then?

We should learn from Nature not only by observation and study but by emptying ourselves. And we empty ourselves when we realize how *little,* rather than how *much,* we know. We empty ourselves by remembering the mystery of Nature. We empty ourselves by Returning to Blue Sky Mind and living in the Mind of Wonder. The Mind of Wonder is attunement itself.

The old guy Lao-tzu talked about the difference between continually accumulating knowledge and the Way of Tao, which is the continual letting go of knowledge. It's the way to become filled, *but not merely with mental debris.* So, to come to this Mind of Wonder, to this attunement, you have to make some room!

To avoid becoming closed and overfull simply hold onto your knowledge, opinions, things, lightly without squeezing too hard. To stay with Blue Sky Mind awhile just hold lightly to the Way like a baby grips a proffered finger. Not too tight. Not too loose.

In the higher stages of the martial arts the true meditation is *receiving.* Emptying to become filled. Returning to stillness in order to act. These aren't just martial art principles — they're for anyone living a life of Practice. Most martial artists think that transmitting, rather than receiving, is the most important thing. But transmitting power, transmitting energy, transmitting mental force is only one part. And it's still a limited way which can't go beyond itself, the real purpose of all ways.

So, *receive*. Become a receiver rather than a transmitter. For maybe the first time in days, weeks, or months, *even years,* the mind stops talking and begins *listening.* This is the reversal of the energy of the mind.

This receiving is the way to Wonder, not the small wonder of mere surprise, but the greater Wonder of Depth, of the Blue Sky Mind. It's opening to the Present. It's a brain which is listening instead of talking. It's to first sense, and then *be* like a mountain stream.

It's to know how to turn and move by seeing a leaf fall in autumn. It's knowing how to relax and become rested by seeing a dormant tree in the winter. It's to intuitively know how to tune into the Creative Source by seeing a bud burst forth with bloom in the spring.

It's all that and more. It's learning *from,* not just *about* Nature. It's learning to listen with your whole being. It's becoming empty. It's the Mind of Wonder. It's becoming wordlessly sculpted by Nature.

You might think that we'd be continually surprised by a life of wonder but that isn't so. Living in not-knowing, the realm of wonder, of infinite possibilities, we're freshened by the unusual, our sense of existence deepened. We're kept on our toes. But we're Returned rather than surprised.

Being surprised often means that we've been knowing a bit too much, with a mind that's a bit too hard, that we've been absent from the mind of wonder. That the realm of infinite possibilities and the Big Changer have become no more than dry thoughts.

The mind of wonder is really the Mind of Readiness. Enlivened but not stuck anywhere. Open, ready, but not for any particular thing. Is that surprising?

ACTION

Action From Stillness

This exercise, the last in Maverick Sutras, will help you to utilize everything that you've read so far. It will acquaint you with "action from stillness," the highest principle of spiritual training.

It is a continuation of the earlier exercise which acquainted us with "non-action," and will further strengthen that tranquil, compulsionless state which can remain as the basis of even the strongest, most powerful actions. Spend some time with "non-action" first.

Return. Pause. Relax. But like a cat instead of a vegetable. Become poised, yet comfortable. Find the Mind of Readiness. Remain there, as if balanced on the brink, yet content to be there. In the words of the Diamond Sutra, "Arouse the mind without placing it anywhere." Become the still point from which the first increment of motion arises, and hang there awhile.

Then ... ACT! Suddenly. Thoroughly. Only this time, choose a different sort of action than before. Don't sweep, don't polish. Instead strike in one swift movement like a hawk. Split a log, hammer a nail, crack an egg. Breath out and become a flash of lightning! Then Return to stillness once again. (Repeat as needed.)

A LIFE OF ACTION

In the end, it all boils down to a life of action. And if people knew that they'd be able to live a life of Practice from the beginning. Instead, most wander the side paths of thought, of *inaction* rather than non-action far too long. Inaction is just hesitation based on confusion. Non-action is action which arises from stillness, action without gaining-mind. A big difference.

So, while many confuse a life of Practice with a life of avoidance, with *thinking* about action, *thinking* about meditation, *thinking* about the principles seen in Nature, only a few know the meaning of non-action, action with nothing-extra. Those few know that a life of Practice, of Depth, is built of actions, real actions, like a wall is built of bricks. You can become one of those few!

Action. There's not so much to say about it, yet it's both the beginning and end of a life of Practice. It's both the calm and the storm together. It's Pure Intent. Total Action. It's reverence for an act of Wonder flashing out of Emptiness. An act which is yours to momentarily revere but never to own.

THE IMMOVABLE

One more time:

> In motion like water
> In stillness like a mirror.

The motionless mind is the best way to move! It's a fact. When action arises from the hidden depths of stillness rather than merely the last fallen domino there's a new quality to your action. But to do this you have to first determine the difference between the Blue Sky Mind and the ephemeral clouds which continually pass on through. Get things straight; which is which?

The beginning of knowing the immovable is knowing how to *pause*. Most people learn to *do* but they never seem to learn to pause. If you can pause both within and without when the tides are pulling all around you, when people are getting excited, you'll find the immovable. Of course, pausing while the mind chatters and chews on things isn't it at all.

The immovable is a Return to Blue Sky Mind coupled with the tendency to remain there. It's the biggest part of Practice. It's to discover the feeling of being unmoved by time without either the pressure to hurry *or* the hesitation of dragging your feet. It's really just balance and, like physical balance, you can only find it on your own, by self-exploration. By knowing the difference between Blue Sky and clouds. And not other people's Blue Sky and clouds but your own!

It takes a lot of pausing, a lot of Returning, a lot of undirected alertness to establish the tendency to remain for a time in the fortress of the immovable, but that's Practice. That's what we're doing! What else are you going to do?

If we're not careful, if we don't have a practice of some sort, or a Good Friend to set us straight, we might look for a balanced state which is incapable of motion, and call *that* the immovable. But that's useless! That's the mistake of double-weighting, of inertia, of inaction. It's the balance of someone lying down. It's balance without poise, without readiness, and it's just not our Way.

So we pause poised! We find in ourselves that balanced state from which we can move easily in any direction both mentally and physically. We find it by ourselves because no one else can find it for us. It's like finding the proper amount to eat — you're on your own!

One of the old guys said:

> When the wooden man sits down to play
> The stone maiden gets up to dance.

That's it! That's that motionless mind that's capable of action we're talking about. Find it. Return to it. Use it. *Visit often!* That's the Practice of the immovable and no one else can do it for you.

A practice really helps. Or a Good Friend. Or maybe a vitally interested spirit will do. Find out! Experiment.

In the martial arts, and really in all life, we find four basic approaches to fear. One is to be overcome by it. "Mommy!" The second is to fight it and force yourself to concentrate on the task at hand. "Whew!" The third is to co-exist with it. Don't fight it. Better. "Sigh!" But the fourth is the Way of Practice. It's to Return to the Blue Sky. It's to find the state of fearlessness, the Blue Sky through which the clouds of fear may blow without harm. "Ahhh!" This is the immovable. It's ... *different.*

To Return to the immovable is to enter a fortress. Yet it's not the ordinary sort of fortress in which we give up mobility for security. It's a place of safety, of calm even if we die. It's the Mind of Readiness, the Mind of the Return. A fortress which is always there for us to use.

But first learn the difference in viewpoint between the Blue Sky and the clouds. Learn to pause. Then learn to act from stillness. Return to the immovable like the wooden man sits down to play. *But don't forget to let the stone maiden dance!*

Find the dynamic balance. The immovable. But do it yourself and don't wait for Tinkerbell to show — because *that* would be inaction! And we don't do that.

ACTION AND THE RETURN

The kind of action which most truly expresses the depth of our spiritual nature is action emerging from stillness. This shouldn't really be a surprise — we see this same mysterious action occurring everywhere in Nature. In the calm before the storm; the flash of lightning in an empty sky. In the dormancy of a tree followed by leaf and flower. In the stillness of a cat and the lazy circling of a hawk before they strike. In the rushing of a mountain stream emerging from the stillness of ice. We see it everywhere we look, but we see it least in the actions of people!

In the world of people we mostly see action emerging from action, or inaction emerging from inaction. But that's living without Flow! Without total action. It's hopping instead of the naturalness of walking. It's sledding instead of skiing. It's thought leading to thought. Words leading to words. It lacks real power because it's not acting totally, from out of Emptiness, like a force of Nature. It's weak, but that's mostly what we see.

Acting from stillness isn't difficult, it's easy, it's natural, it's nothing-extra. What's difficult, what's missing, is *stillness emerging from action!* You'll never come to total action, true action, unless you Return to the poised stillness of Emptiness first. That's the crux. Then, and only then, do action and stillness both become meditation. Not self-consciousness but real meditation. Rolling with the Mirror, letting forces build and then releasing them. Cleanly, purely, from the depths of intuition instead of contrivance. That's Practice. That's the Return. That's the way to act like a force of Nature. Action from stillness from action from stillness from action from stillness. Always conforming to the changing rhythm of the Greater Rhythm. Adjusting to the Flow.

If we don't Return first in order to act, in order to be *poised* to act in the Mind of Readiness, our actions lose both grace and power. Our will opposes the Flow, our muscles oppose our movement. Action becomes muddled instead of clear. Our flexors and extensors quarrel rather than cooperate, and tension results. We can rush forward or we can hesitate; we can hurry or drag our feet, but that's about it. *So we have to act as if the deed were done and yet wait as if there were no deed to do!* That's really Returning. And really acting too.

So, just as this total action is the kind of true action which best expresses our spiritual nature, this poised, vital stillness is the kind of stillness which truly expresses that nature too. It's the stillness of surface tension, the right amount of tension with depth below.

Acting from stillness is wonderful. But it's only half. Return in order to act and you have it all. It takes trust in the Flow. In *both* aspects of the Flow. Look into it. It's not easy at first but it's definitely worth your while.

SAYING AND DOING

Here's a big one. One that puts everything about a life of Practice in perspective. A bottom line that makes things clearer. Because it's easy to talk. It's even easy to talk about the Way. About Practice. Particularly easy, in fact. But if it's only talk then the Way is really less than a way and Practice is reduced to something far less than practice. And Action, the kind of Action which concerns us, can't be found anywhere around.

So, this is important. It's about Saying and Doing. It's not too hard to understand, and it's also not too interesting to most people. Most would rather hear about meditation, about emptiness, stories about the old guys, almost anything besides Saying and Doing.

But a life of Practice is something far more than mere philosophy, more than simply coming up with yet another way of defining the Rolling Mirror. Practice is a life of *Action,* a vital life of participation in the Way. A life lived from the inside out, from stillness to action, which may include, but isn't based on, any form of intellection at all.

Saying and Doing. Important? Yes, but, like commitment, not too popular these days. Not too popular at all.

Saying and Doing isn't always easy, but without it you don't really have much. It just means that you try to live according to the principles which become evident in your own Practice. *As they become evident.* It means your words and deeds become closer rather than farther apart as time goes on. It means that the depth of your actions increases as the depth of your understanding increases.

But don't run off the other side of the road! Don't expect to live a life with no mistakes. You *will* make mistakes because clear seeing follows the observation of the results of action. It's not just Returning to act — it's acting to Return also! It's not just Returning, it's going forth too. So you *will* make mistakes. And no, enlightenment, or whatever you like to call it, won't insure a mistake free life. No way. Forget it.

The other thing is your words and actions can never be perfectly one with no deviation. This is due to the misleading nature of words and the unpredictability of the results of action in the Rolling Mirror. The Big Changer. It's due to cloudy days. It's due to "seeing through a glass darkly." But the ever-whispered request of Practice is that we come *closer.* And closer. Words and deeds. Saying and Doing. You have to remember it's like driving, not something you just get once and for all, it takes attention and adjustment from now on.

And it's like balance. You have to find a way to make Saying and Doing an integral part of your Practice, and of your life, without becoming either too rigid or too lax. Without becoming attached, you *just do it.* When it's time to re-adjust, get back in the right lane, *you just do it.* You do it because Practice is more than just philosophy.

You do it because actions speak louder than words. You do it because you're trying to understand the Way of Action. *Through acting!* It's nothing to get puffed up about. But nothing to forget about either.

So, don't make a big thing about it even though it *is* important. Just let your words and deeds move a little closer together. Start easy. You know, do what you say you'll do or don't say you'll do it. That's a start. Then use the principles of Practice without becoming attached to them. Without turning them into rules. Be a student rather than a teacher. Even if you're a teacher! *Especially if you're a teacher!*

Here's a hint how to do it. Don't hurry up to go meditate because that's just not the way it's done! Even if no one else notices, *you* will. And that's enough. Steer. Balance. Closer ... closer. Do everything like that. Or as much as you can. But don't make it into a chore. It's not. It's just Saying and Doing. It's just part of a life of Action. A *big* part.

BEYOND NAME AND GAIN

As long as you're still controlled by the big bosses of name and gain you can't be free. As long as you have a price for parting with your Blue Sky Mind, you can be bought too cheaply. And, unlike your good, solid, business transaction, when you let the big bosses interfere you may find yourself selling out for mere dreams and empty promises.

Nothing is worth the price of giving up your Blue Sky Mind. Nothing you can get done; nothing you think about; nothing you gain thereby; nothing you can get known for doing. That's it. That's going beyond name and gain. That's real beyondness. That's "gone, gone, gone beyond," and it's the never-fail doorway to Practice. It's to arrive intact in the unpressured Blue Sky Mind in one exhalation. You have to see the truth of it, see that it's really so, or else the big bosses will just keep riding you.

The moment Practice becomes tainted with ideas of gain it becomes reduced to practice — just repetition and accumulation. But when practice, *whatever your practice is,* loses the pressure of gaining-mind, then Practice emerges instantly. And it only takes the smallest touch of gaining-mind to reduce Practice to practice, depth to shallowness, the Panorama to tunnel vision. It's the same way the smallest touch of gaining-mind taints generosity, the smallest bit of unnoticed attachment taints clarity. One of the old guys said, "the difference of a tenth of an inch and heaven and earth are rent asunder," and that's just about it.

So keep a sharp eye on not only the coarse urges to gain this or that, to be known by others as this or that, but also watch for the subtle desire to become anything other than what you really are *right now*. Because that can taint your Practice. That slight bit of pressure may keep you from the natural joy of the unpressured state. May make you stare at clouds until you forget about the sky.

This unpressured state isn't just for being light, airy and mellow. *It's simply the best way to do anything at all.* It's acting so you don't oppose yourself with the tension of wanting. This "beyondness," beyond name and gain, is the key to Action. If it's just ordinary action you want, getting things done, gaining this or that, then forget all this. Hang out with the big bosses and call it a day. Or a life. But if you want to do things in a totally different way, without pressure, acting from out of stillness instead of agitation, well, then you can't afford to pass this up.

Beyondness. Very easy to understand. Pressure, no pressure. Clouds, sky. And pretty easy to do once or twice. But as a way of life? That's Practice, and that's pretty hard. But that doesn't mean that it's impossible. Just decide that your Blue Sky Mind isn't for sale at any price. Then even if you get cloudy you'll clear up before too long. And it may be hard, but it's still easier than always having the big bosses on your back. Right?

ACTING WITHOUT ACTING

The logical mind hears about non-action, or non-effort, and manages to come up with something which is really just lethargy, or laziness. It might conjure up a picture of "spiritual" people, maybe the old guys, meditating, doing nothing, or even getting things done with the use of mental rather than physical force. But that has nothing to do with non-action!

Because non-action is a way of acting! Non-action is the highest quality action of all. It's the Way of the Tao. It's the way things work in Nature. It's not the kind of doing nothing which is really just stagnation, it's the kind of doing nothing which is acting with nothing-extra. Non-action simply means non-ownership of action. When we can simply act without the burdensome sense of ownership of "our" actions, our actions become pure, that extra speediness and tension is dropped and our work becomes effortless because we cease opposing ourselves. Our actions flow with the Greater Flow. Non-action isn't *laziness;* it's the way the old guys did things and it's the way we should too!

When we act without this sense of ownership an interesting thing happens: we act as if there is no actor! We act as purely, as unselfconsciously as a flower blooming in spring. We simply supply the concurrent causes to get things done and then allow things to get done.

Most people can only do this or that, one or the other: They can hurry or they can drag their feet, they can become personally involved and do a good job *or* they can be aloof and not give it their best shot. But either of these approaches has nothing at all to do with Practice. The Way of Practice is altogether different and involves entering totally, giving each task everything you have *except the extra tension generated by the feeling of ownership, of over-concern with results, of the feeling, "I am the doer of it all."*

That's Practice and that's non-action too. It's the way to do things purely without being tainted by gaining-mind. It's the only way to act so that the will does not oppose the Flow. It's easy. But it's also easy to lose it in an instant. There are, however, a couple of sure-fire ways to get it down.

One is that each act is entered totally and then put behind you without self-congratulation at all. The other is even easier — it's to esteem the wonderful and mysterious action of the Flow instead of just your own part in things.

And then, what are you really left with? You're left with the Tao. With the mysterious action of an unfolding flower. You may not gain much, but you're left with the flow of the Greater Flow.

Is that enough? It's up to you.

Many people think that stillness is the end of Practice, and it's easy to see where they get that idea. But stillness is the beginning of Practice. You can't hang out there. There's more to do.

Action is the culmination of Practice. But it's how you act, the quality of that action which is important and which transforms practice into Practice. It's non-action. It's action emerging from stillness which is important. It's acting without delusion as to the nature and results of your action, yet still acting anyway! It's dynamic, it's taking principles into your life and using them. But using them without owning them. Without turning them into rules.

Return in order to act. Discover action from stillness from action from stillness from action from stillness. Might as well go first class. Can you do it? Can you un-do it? Sure you can. Start today!

EPILOGUE:
THE LAST HARANGUE

A Life of Practice, Depth, Clarity, Flow, Wonder and Action. That's some life! And they're all simply aspects of the same Blue Sky Mind. That's important to see.

But when attachment arises it's all just clouds. When attachment takes hold the right way becomes the wrong way, every time, and in a heartbeat. Luckily, we have the ability to Return and to let things naturally come back into balance once again, to drop attachment and flow with the Greater Flow. That's *Returning* – not being right but righting yourself. Finding your poise and balance in this often precarious sphere of the Rolling Mirror.

Being sharp without becoming small is an art, and resting more and more in the Mind of Readiness is the secret of that art. Then you won't get caught by things. Even things like this! And then you're *doing* it, which is way better than *getting* it.

And forget about "enlightenment." Enlightenment's not enough! It's like one breath, or one meal – it's only enough when succeeded by many others. So, like breathing, eating ... enlightening.

Enlightening! That's the Way for us. It's Returning, over and over again. That's our kind of Practice. And the way to all the other things too! It's enough enlightenments, enough Returns, to make up a whole life.

You can't know everything! That's a fact. But not-knowing can teach you more than you ever dreamed of. Open-mindedness can create a much larger world than you ever imagined. So learn the kind of knowing that's *doing* what you know instead of merely thinking your brains out. No one else can do this for you.

Maybe you'll have a Good Friend, and maybe you won't. Maybe it'll be easy sometimes, and maybe it'll be hard. That's not the important part, that's just clouds. The important part is not to just hang out waiting for your fairy-godmother! And here's the biggest hint, and the last one of all:

Just get on with it!

Books by G. BlueStone

Maverick Sutras

Enlightening

Light of the Kensei

Journeys on Mind Mountain

Life in the Rolling Mirror

Ask for these titles at your favorite
bookstore or, for a complimentary
catalog, write or call today:

Avant Press
Post Office Box 8095
Durango, Colorado
81301-0202 USA
ph. 800-243-2259